£2.50

THE LIBRARY

University of Ulster at Magee

Due Back (subject to recall)

Fines will apply to items returned after due date

John Weaver

Orchesography

Translated from the French of Feuillet

AND

A Small Treatise
of Time and Cadence
in Dancing

London 1706

1971
Gregg International Publishers Limited

Orchesography is reproduced from a copy
in the library of Mrs. Raymond Lister

ISBN 0 576 28201 4

Republished in 1971 by Gregg International Publishers Limited
Westmead, Farnborough, Hants, England

Printed in England

ORCHESOGRAPHY.

OR, THE

ART

OF

DANCING,

BY

Characters and *Demonstrative Figures.*

WHEREIN

The whole *Art* is explain'd; with compleat
Tables of all *Steps* us'd in *Dancing*, and *Rules* for the
Motions of the *Arms*, &c.

WHEREBY

Any Person (who understands *Dancing*) may of himself
learn all manner of *Dances.*

BEING

An Exact and Just *Translation* from the
French of Monsieur *Feuillet.*

By JOHN WEAVER, *Dancing-Master.*

Pars pedibus plaudunt Choreas, ———
Virg. Æneid. 6.

LONDON: Printed by *H. Meere*, at the *Black Fryar*, in *Black
Fryars*, for the Author, and are to be Sold by *P. Valliant, French* Bookseller,
near *Catherine-Street*, in the *Strand.* 1706.

To Mr. Ifaac.

S I R,

THO' *Dancing* and *Mufick* feem to be of near an equal Antiquity, and even of an equal Extent, yet *Mufick* has long receiv'd an Advantage, which *Dancing* wanted. *Mufick* has employ'd the Pens of many of the Learned, both Ancient and Modern, and has had the Benefit of an univerfal Character, which convey'd the harmonious Compofitions to all Lovers of the *Art* in all Nations. *Dancing*, on the contrary, tho' celebrated by Ancient Authors in an extraordinary

A 2

manner,

The DEDICATION. *Praises*

manner, and with uncommon Phrafes, (as I
fhall fhew in a Treatife, which I fhall fuddenly
publifh on that Subject) yet among the Mo-
derns, it has been wholly unknown to the
Learned, and deftitute of all Pens, in either the
fpeculative or practick part of the *Art*, which
for want of an univerfal Character, was confin'd
to the immediate Mafter and Scholar, or at fartheft, to a narrow traditional Inftruction, which
none could participate of without a Teacher,
who had been taught by fome other, either
Compofer, or Scholar of fuch Compofer. This
Inconvenience at length ftirr'd up Monfieur
Beauchamp to begin what Monfieur *Feuillet* ac-
complifh'd in the following Treatife, which tho'
for fome time enjoy'd by the *French* Nation, as
a native Growth, *now firft appears* in its true
and juft Extent in its Tranfplantation into the
Englifh Climate and Language.

   THE Service to the Lovers and Profeffors
of this *Art*, having been the chief Motive of
my Undertaking fo difficult a Province, that we
who enjoy the Happinefs of fo Great a Mafter as
Mr. *Ifaac*, fhould not want the Advantage of
fpreading that Excellence in this *Art*, which
renders him fo admir'd by all who have any
Tafte of it ; fo having receiv'd fuch great and
generous

The DEDICATION.

generous Encouragement in this Study from you, Sir; the Product of that Encouragement and Study does, as it were, out of a natural Right and juft Gratitude, feek Shelter under your Patronage, and challenge the Advantage of appearing in the World under the Protection of your Name, whofe known Judgment and Maftery in this *Art*, will fecure me from the Cenfure of Malice and Ignorance.

HOWEVER, I fhall have little to fear, if I am fo happy as to merit that generous Affiftance, which you have been pleafed to give me in the compiling of this Book ; and I am apt to flatter my felf, that I have done the Original that Juftice, that the Author will have no Reafon to complain : But whatever Defects I may have been guilty of in it, I promife my felf Forgivenefs from fo much Goodnefs and Candor, as all People (with Juftice) allow to Mr. *Ifaac*. You are fo truly diftinguifh'd from moft Men, by a peculiar Sincerity and Zeal for the Service of your Friend, or him whom you have once thought fit to efpoufe, that as I have done nothing but comply'd with my own Inclination, in offering this publick Acknowledgment of your Favour, fo I have infinite Caufe of being perfectly fatisfy'd with my Patron.

I

The DEDICATION.

I KNOW it is the Cuſtom of *Dedicators,* to launch forth into the Praiſes of the Virtues and Parts of their Patrons ; but I know Mr. *Iſaac* too well, to think I can render my ſelf more acceptable to him, by entertaining him with his own Deſerts, ſince they are too well known to all your Acquaintance, to need a Publication in this place. Not but that it would be a Theme infinitely grateful to me ; but I ſhall curb that Inclination, and deny my ſelf a Pleaſure that would be diſguſtful to you. It is enough, that by ſpreading the Knowledge which the following Book conveys, your Excellence in the *Art,* your admirable Compoſitions will more eaſily, and more largely encreaſe the Number of your Admirers ; among which, there never will be one more truly devoted to your Service, than,

SIR,

Your moſt Obliged

Humble Servant,

John Weaver.

PREFACE.

I Perſwade my ſelf, that before ſo uſeful a Curioſity as the following Treatiſe, it would not be diſagreeable to the Reader,
to give him an Account of the Origin and Progreſs of the Art
of Orcheſography. Furetier, *in his Hiſtorical Dictionary,*
tells us of a curious Treatiſe of this Art by one Thoinet Arbeau, *print-*
ed 1588, *at* Langres, *from whom Monſieur* Feuillet, *in his Preface,*
ſuppoſes this Art to date its firſt Riſe and Birth, tho' he could never
procure a Sight of it, as not to be found in Paris. *But this very Book*
falling into my Hands, I took Care to peruſe it with ſome Attenti-
on, but found it far ſhort of that Expectation, which ſuch Recom-
mendation had rais'd in me : For tho' it might perhaps have given
the Hint to Mr. Beauchamp; *yet it is nothing but an imperfect*
rough Draught, nor is it confin'd to Dancing , ſince it treats be-
ſides of beating the Drum, playing on the Pipe, and the like.
  But notwithſtanding this blind Hint of Arbeau, *to do Juſtice to*
Monſ. Beauchamp, *we muſt attribute to him the Invention of this*
Art, who in all Probability, could no more ſee the former Book, than
Monſ. Feuillet. *But as no Art was ever invented and perfected at*
once ; ſo it remain'd for Monſ. Feuillet, *to raiſe the compleat and*
finiſh'd Superſtructure on Monſ. Beauchamp's *Foundation ; and it*
muſt be allowed, that Monſ. Feuillet *has carry'd this Art to a very*
great Perfection, and taken a great deal of Pains in the Improve-
ment of the Character, and given Rules ſo juſt, and a Method ſo
proper, that I cannot imagine any Man can flatter himſelf with an
Ability of deſigning a better, or more regular manner. For this
Reaſon I choſe rather to follow his Method entirely, than attempt
any Alteration of my own, which I have done with that Care
and Diligence, that I think I may aſſure the Reader I have o-
mitted nothing that he has deliver'd. I have alſo made it my Buſi-
neſs

The PREFACE.

nefs to bring the Reader acquainted with the Meaning of my Author, as well as his Words, which is a Happinefs every Tranflator has not the Power of arriving at, as generally either ignorant of the Subject or Language he tranflates from, or into, or both.

Another Fault of our common Tranflators I have avoided with all the Induftry I could : Some of them pretending to meddle with Books of Art, and not underftanding the Terms of Art, give us fuch an odd Jargon, that we can never underftand it without the Interpretation of a Mafter, or having Recourfe to the Original it felf. I have therefore render'd all the French Terms into Englifh, but with fo much Caution of doing Juftice to the Author, and the Art, that I would not depend on my own Judgment, but let none pafs without the Approbation of the beft Englifh Mafters.

The Perfection, which Dancing is now come to in England, feems to point this Time out as the fitteft Juncture, for the Publication of a Book of this Nature; fince we now enjoy in this Nation, Performers and Mafters of greater Excellence than any other part of Europe; who fhew every Beauty of the Art in its full Glory and Perfection. For whoever fhall confider the Mafterly Compofitions of Ball-Dances by Mr. Ifaac, which are fo well adapted to the manner of our School-teaching, (peculiar to England, no other Nation having any fuch thing as publick Dancing-Schools) whoever fhall fee the admirable Compofitions of Monf. L' Abbe in Ballet, and his Performance, with that of M.Defbargues, M.Du Ruel, and M.Cherrier, can hope to fee nothing in this Art of greater Excellence, unlefs any wonderful Genius fhould arife, and advance this once celebrated Art to that Perfection, which drew the Eyes, and employ'd the Pens of the old Greeks and Romans ; a lively Defcription of which, the Reader may fee in this Epigram, by an unknown Hand.

Mafcula fœmineo derivans Pectora Sexu,
   Atq; aptans lentum Sexum at utrumq; latus,
Egreffus Scenam Populum faltator adorat
  Solerti pendet prodere verba Manu.

Nam

The PREFACE.

Nam cum grata Chorus diffundit cantica dulcis
  Quæ refonat Cantor, motibus ipfe probat.
Pugnat, ludit, amat, Bacchatur, Vertitur, adftat,
  Illuftrat verum, cuncta decore replet.
Tot Linguæ, quot Membra viro, Mirabilis eft Ars,
  Quæ facit Articulos voce filente loqui.

*From this Epigram, it is plain, that the ancient Dancing had
something more than Motion, Meafure, and Figure, and exprefs'd
the Paffions and Actions of Mankind, was a fort of filent Poetry,
and the Painting, tho' without Colours, fo expreffive, as to touch
and charm every Beholder.*

*There will be no need to enforce the Ufe of this Art, and by Con-
fequence recommend the Book that teaches it, to all Lovers of Dancing, fince it carries its own Evidence with it felf, and has already convinc'd them of its Benefit and Advantage ; and I queftion not
but others will find the fame Satisfaction from their Study, which I
have done, fince by a clofe Application to this Character, I have made
fuch a Progrefs in it, as to be able to communicate all Dances to
the reft of the Profeffion at any Diftance.   I have a great deal of
Reafon to believe, that had not I firft undertaken to make Monf.
Feuillet fpeak Englifh, this Character had yet a longer while remain'd a Secret to this Nation ; thofe who had made their private
Market of it, not being willing to admit any Rivals in an Art, which
chiefly diftinguifh'd them from others of their Profeffion.*

*I muft undeceive fome, who may perhaps miftake the Defign of
the following Treatife, and take it for an Inftruction, or fome Im-
provement in the Art of Dancing, or Method of Teaching.   But
I muft affure them, that I am not yet Mafter of Vanity enough to
venture upon a Task fo difficult, and fo invidious, fince I am of
Opinion, that there are not better Mafters for inftructing Scholars in
a genteel Movement and Addrefs, than the Englifh.*

*I fhall not therefore detain the Reader any longer in the Porch,
but leave him now to enter, and improve.*

Ingredere ut proficias.

a   A

A List of the *Dancing-Masters,*
Subscribers to this Undertaking.

A

Monsieur L' Abbe.

B

Mr. Bosely *of* Norwich.

C

Mr. Tho. Caverly.
Mr. Ant. Caverly.
Monsieur Camille.
Monsieur Cherrier.
Mr. Claxton.
Mr. Couch.
Monsieur Cottin.
Mr. Counley *of* Barbadoes.
Mr. Cragg.
Mr. Christian.

D

Monsieur Debargues.
Mr. Delamain *of* Dublin.
Monsieur Le Duc.
Mr. Douson.

E

Monsieur D' Elisle.
Mr. Essex.

G

Mr. Groscourt.
Mr. Gery.

H

Mr. Walter Holt, *Sen.*
Mr. Walter Holt, *Jun.*
Mr. Rich. Holt.
Mr. Heale *of* Salisbury.

I

Mr. Isaac.

L

Mr. Lally.
Mr. Char. Lewis.

N

Mr. Nicholson.

O

Mr. Orlabeer.

P

Mr. Pawlet.
Mr. Pemberton.
Mr. Porter *of* Darby.
Mr. Pritton.

R

Monsieur Du Ruell.
Mr. Rogers.

S

Monsieur Serancour.
Monsieur L' Sac.
Mr. Sexton *of* York.
Mr. Shirley.

This Undertaking has also been encouraged by the Subscriptions of several of the Nobility and Gentry

E R R A T A.

Dedication, page 2. line 1. for *Phrases,* read *Praises.* P. 8. l. 3. f. *the,* r. *a.* P. 17. l. 3, f. *afterwards,* r. *forwards.* P. 34. l. 7. after *Page,* add *as E F do the upper end of the Room, G H the lower part.* P. 40. l. 2. f. *behind,* r. *before.* P. 47. l. 4. f. *Rigaudons,* r. *Rigaudons.*

Orchefography.

OR,

The ART of

DANCING

BY

Chara&ters and Demonftrative Figures.

By which any Perfon, who underftands Dancing, *may of himfelf eafily learn all manner of* Dances.

THE *Explanation* of the *Terms* belonging to *DANCING*, feem to be altogether needlefs, fince they are fo plain and intelligible of themfelves : But left the Reader fhould put wrong Conftruĉtions on thofe *Terms* of *Art* which the *Dancing-Mafters* make ufe of, I fhall give the following *Explanation* of them.

Dancing

Dancing is compofed of *Pofitions*, *Steps*, *Sinkings*, *Rifings*, *Springings*, *Capers*, *Fallings*, *Slidings*, *Turnings* of the Body, *Cadence* or *Time*, *Figures*, &c.

Pofitions, are the different Placings of the Feet in Dancing.

Steps, are the Motions of the Feet from one place to another.

Sinkings, are the Bendings of the Knees.

Rifings, are when we rife from a *Sink*, or erect our felves.

Springing, is a *rifing* or leaping from the Ground.

Capers, are when in *rifing* or leaping from the Ground, one Leg beats againft the other, which we call *Cutting*.

Fallings, are when the Body, being out of its proper Poife, falls by its own Weight.

Slidings, are when, in *moving*, the Foot flides on the Ground.

Turnings, are when the Body turns either one way or the other.

Cadence or *Time*, is a right underftanding of the different Meafures, and Obfervation of the moft remarkable places in the *Tune*.

Figures, are *Tracts* made by *Art*, on which the *Dancer* is to move.

Before I proceed to demonftrate what I have already explain'd, I fhall defcribe the *Room* or *Stage*, where *Dancing* is perform'd ; as alfo the different *Tracts* or *Figures* to be made thereon, and the *Pofture* and *Prefence of the Body*, in which the *Performer* ought to ftand.

Of

Of the Stage, Room, or School.

THE *Stage* or *Dancing-Room,* I fhall reprefent by an *Oblong,* as in the Figure A B C D, of which the upper end is A B, the lower end C D; the right fide B D, and the left fide A C.

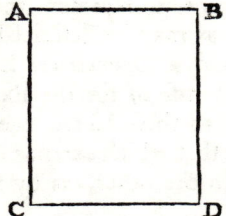

The Prefence of the Body.

THE *Pofture* or Prefence of the Body, is to have refpect to that part of the *Room,* to which the Face or Fore-part of the Body is directed, which I defcribe by the Figure F G H I, of which F G fhews the two Sides of the Body, H the Face or Fore-part, and I the Back or Hinder-part.

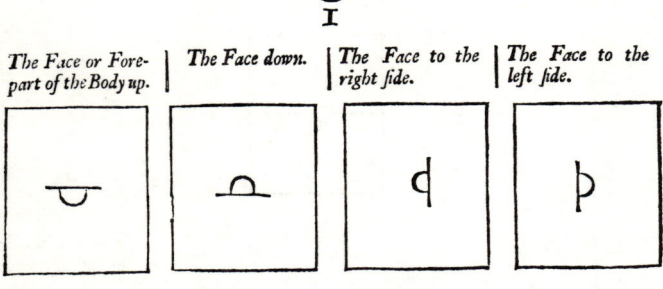

The Face or Fore-part of the Body up.	The Face down.	The Face to the right fide.	The Face to the left fide.

Of the Tract.

THE Line on which the Dances are defcribed, I call the *Tract.*

Which *Tract* ferves for two Ends, the firft to direct the *Steps* and *Pofitions,* and the other to reprefent the Figure of the *Dance.*

All *Steps* and *Pofitions* may be defcribed upon two Lines, *viz.* upon a *Right* Line, and a *Diametrical* Line ; but becaufe the *Tract* muft alfo be made ufe of for the Explanation of the Figure of *Dances,* I fhall add to thefe Lines, the *Circular* and *Oblique.*

A *Right Line,* I call that which extends it felf in Length, from one end of the *Room* to the other, as by the Line mark'd K.

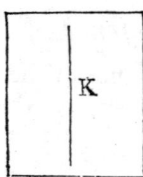

A *Diametrical Line,* is that which goes crofs the *Room* from fide to fide, as is fhewn by the Line L.

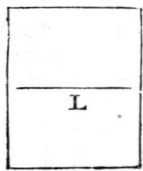

The

The *Circular Line*, is that which goes round the *Room*, as is exprefs'd by the Letter M.

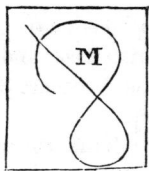

The *Oblique Line*, is that which goes crofs the *Room*, from Corner to Corner, as may be feen by the Line N.

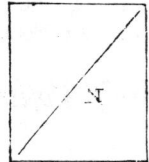

Every one of thefe *Lines*, or *Tracts*, may jointly or feparately form the *Figure* of a *Dance*, on which may be defcribed the *Pofitions* and *Steps*, as in *Figure* O. The beginning of which *Tract*, is fhewn by the *Character* reprefenting the *Pofture* or *Prefence of the Body*, which muft be join'd to it, to fhew the *Pofition* of the Body at the beginning of the *Dance*.

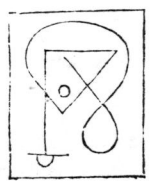

Of the Positions.

THere are ten Sorts of *Positions* generally us'd in *Dancing*, which are divided into *True* and *False*.

The *True*, are when the Feet are plac'd uniform, and have the Toes turn'd out equally.

The *False*, are some of them uniform, others not, and differ from the *True*, in that, the Toes are turn'd inward, or one in, and the other out.

In all *Positions* whatsoever, the Form of the Foot is known by these Marks, *viz*. That which resembles an o, represents the Heel; the Line join'd to it, the Ankle; and the Extremity of that Line, the Point of that Foot.

A half Position.

The Toe
The Ankle
The Heel

This Figure of the *Foot*, is but a half *Position*, because it represents but one *Foot*, whereas a whole *Position* does that of two, as in the Figure A B.

Position.

'Tis to be observ'd, that the Letter A, in the foregoing Figure, represents the left *Foot*, and B, the right.

Of

Of true Pofitions.

THere are five true *Pofitions.* The firft is when the two Feet are join'd together, the Heels being one againft the other.

Firft Pofition.

The fecond is when the Feet are open, or feparate, on a Line, one diftant from the other the length of the Foot.

Second Pofition.

The third is when the Heel of one Foot is join'd to the Ankle of the other, which I fhall hereafter term *inclos'd.*

Third Pofition.

The fourth is when the two Feet are plac'd one before the other, the diftance of a Foot in length.

Fourth Pofition.

The fifth is when the two Feet are crofs'd, the Heel of one directly oppofite to the Toe of the other.

Fifth Pofition.

Of

The Art of Dancing.
Of falſe Poſitions.

THere are alſo five of theſe.   The firſt is when the **Toes**
are turn'd inwards, and touch each other, the **Heels** being open on the Line.   *Firſt Poſition.*

The ſecond is when the **Toes** are turn'd inwards, there being the diſtance of a **Foot's Length** between the **Toes** ;   the
Heels as before.   *Second Poſition.*

The third is when the **Toe** of one **Foot** is outwards, and the
other inwards, the one parallel towards the other.
                 Third   Poſition.

The fourth is when the **Toes** are turn'd inwards , ſo that
the **Toe** of one **Foot** points to the **Ankle** of the other.
                 Fourth \   *Poſition.*

The fifth *falſe Poſition*, is mark'd like the fifth true one,
and ſeems to be the ſame *Poſition* ; but notwithſtanding, they are
very different, for whereas in the true one, the **Toes** are turn'd
outwards, in the falſe, they are turn'd inwards, croſſing each
other, ſo that the **Heel** of one **Foot** is right againſt the **Toe** of
the other,   and is to be diſtinguiſh'd from the true one by a
ſmall Bar between the *Poſition.*
                 Fifth | *Poſition.*

Altho'

Of Steps.

AAtho' *Steps* made ufe of in Dancing, are almoft innumerable, I fhall neverthelefs reduce them to five, which ferve to exprefs the different Figures the Leg makes in moving : Thefe I fhall call, a *ftraight plain Step*, an *open Step*, a *circular* or *round Step*, a *waving Step*, and a *beaten Step*.

A *ftraight Step*, is when the Foot moves in a right Line ; which is to be made two ways, forwards, and backwards.

The *open Step*, is when the Leg opens ; which is to be done three ways, one outwards, another inwards, both which make an Arch or half Circle, and the third fideways, which may alfo be called a *ftraight Step*, becaufe the Motion of it is in a direct Line.

The *round* or *circular Step*, is when the Foot, in moving, makes a *circular Figure* ; of this there is two ways, one outwards, and another inwards.

The *waving Step*, is when the Foot, in moving, turns both inwards and outwards. There are three ways of doing this, forwards, backwards, and fideways.

The *beaten Step*, is when one Leg or Foot is beaten againft the other. Of this there are alfo three ways of performing, *viz.* forwards, backwards, and fideways.

A *Step* is known by the Character following, *viz.* a black Spot mark'd A, reprefenting the *Pofition* of the *Foot*, the Line drawn from that Spot, mark'd B, fhewing the *Motion, Figure,* and *Largnefs* of the *Step*, as from A to D, and laftly, by a fmall fide Stroke join'd to the End of the Line C, reprefenting the Foot, of which D is the Heel, and E the Point of the Foot, or Toe.

E
D C
B
A   C   A

A Demonſtration of all the *Steps* which have been before explain'd.

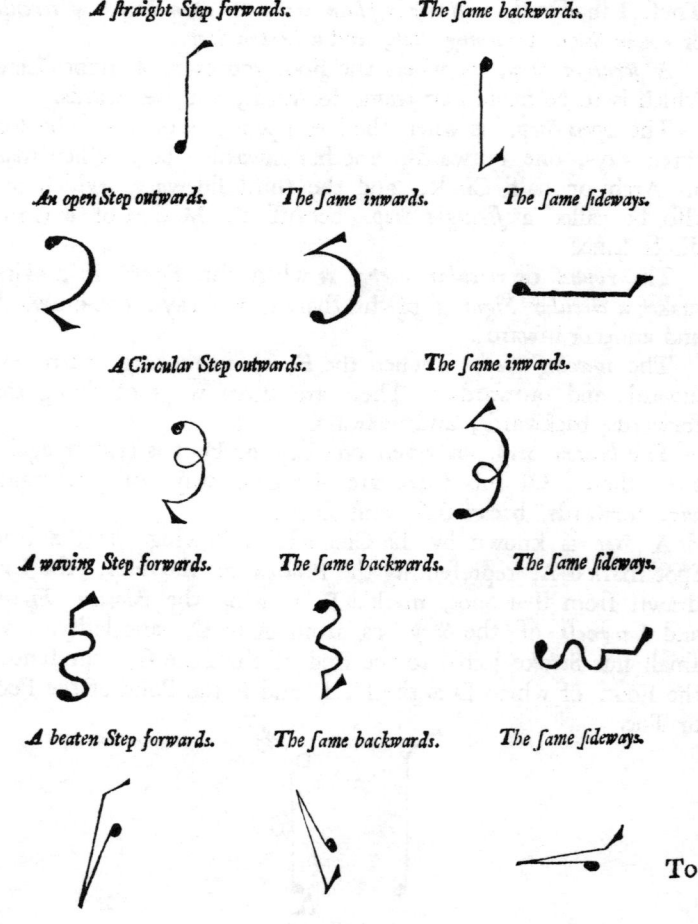

A ſtraight Step forwards.   *The ſame backwards.*

An open Step outwards.   *The ſame inwards.*   *The ſame ſideways.*

A Circular Step outwards.   *The ſame inwards.*

A waving Step forwards.   *The ſame backwards.*   *The ſame ſideways.*

A beaten Step forwards.   *The ſame backwards.*   *The ſame ſideways.*

To

To a *Step* may be added thefe following Marks, *viz. Sinking, Rifing, Springing* or *Bounds, Capers, Falling, Sliding, holding the Foot up, Pointing* the *Toes, placing* the *Heel, turning* a *quater Turn,* a *half Turn,* a *three quarter Turn,* and a *whole Turn.*

The Mark for a *Sink,* is a little Stroke inclining towards the little black Head.

A Sink.

The Mark for a *Rife* from a *Sink,* is when there is a little ftraight Stroke upon the *Step.*

A Rife.

The Mark of a *Spring* or *Rife* from the Ground, is when there are two of the aforefaid Strokes, which is fometimes call'd a *Bound.*

A Spring, or Bound.

The Mark for a *Caper,* is when there are three Strokes.

A Caper.

The

The Mark for a *Falling Step*, is when at the End of the little ſtraight Stroke, another ſtraight one is join'd parallel to the *Step*, and pointing to the Mark for the *Foot*.

A falling Step.

The Mark of a *Slide*, is when at the End of the little Stroke, a ſmall Bar is plac'd parallel to the *Step*.

A Slide.

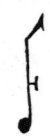

The Mark for the *Foot up*, is when the *Step* is cut off.

The Foot up.

The Mark for *pointing* the *Foot*, without the Body's bearing upon it, is when there is a *Point* directly at the End of that which repreſents the *Toe*.

To point the Foot.

'The

The Mark for placing the *Heel,* without the Body's bearing upon it, is when there is a *Point* directly behind that which reprefents the *Heel.*

To place the Heel.

A *quarter Turn* of the Body, is fhewn by a quarter of a *Circle* plac'd on the *Step.*

A quarter Turn.

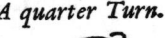

A *half Turn,* is reprefented by a *half Circle.*

A half Turn.

A *three quarter Turn,* is fhewn by a *three quarter Circle.*

A three quarter Turn.

A *whole Turn,* is reprefented by a *whole Circle.*

A whole Turn.

Steps

Steps may have several Marks.

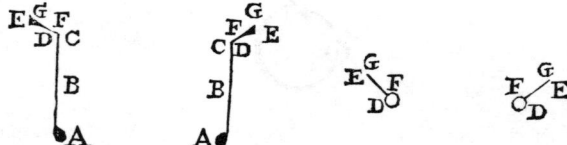

Sink and Rise.	Rise and Sink.	Sink and Bound	Bound and Sink	Sink, Bound, and Sink.	Sink and Caper

Rise and Fall.	Sink, Rise, and Slide.	Sink and Hop.	Sink, Bound, and Turn.	Sink, Rise, and point the Toe.	Sink, Bound, & place the Heel.

How to place the Marks in their proper Order.

IT is neceſſary firſt to know, that a *Step* has three Diviſions, *viz.* a *Beginning*, *Middle*, and *End* : You muſt alſo conſider the Foot, as well in *Steps* as *Poſitions*, has two Sides, an Inſide and an Outſide. The Beginning of the *Step*, is the Beginning of the Line, joining the little black Spot, as is ſhewn by the Letter A. The Middle, is the middle of the Line, as at Letter B. And the End, is the Extremity of the Line, joining that which repreſents the Foot, as at Letter C. The Outſide of the Foot, is between the Heel and the end of the little Toe, mark'd D E ; and the Inſide, is that which is between the Heel and End of the great Toe, as is mark'd F G.

There

There are three ways of *Sinking, viz.* before the Foot moves, in moving, and after it has moved.

When there is the Mark of a *Sink* at the beginning of a *Step,* the *Sink* muft be made before the Foot moves.

Sink before the Foot moves.

When the *Sink* is mark'd in the middle of the *Step,* the *Sink* is not to be made 'till the Foot has made half the *Step.*

A Sink in moving.

When the *Sink* is mark'd at the end of the *Step,* the *Sink* muft not be made 'till the *Step* is finifh'd.

A Sink after Movement.

It is the fame thing in the Marks of a Rife.

Rife before the Foot moves. | *Rife in moving.* | *Rife after Movement.*

Sink

| Sink and Rife before the Foot moves. | Sink and Rife in moving. | Sink and Rife after moving. |

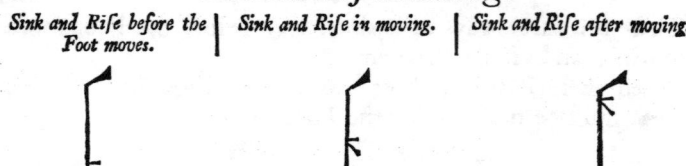

| Sink before Moving, and Rife in Moving. | Sink as before, and Rife after Moving. | Sink in Moving, Rife after the Movement. |

Obfervations upon Springings.

SPringings may be perform'd two ways, viz. with both Feet at once, or with one Foot only.

The *Springings* which are made on both Feet, are mark'd upon the *Pofitions*, as hereafter will appear ; whereas the *Springings* that are made in moving, are mark'd upon the *Steps*, as has been already fhewn, and will again appear by the Sequel.

Of fpringing Steps.

A *Springing Step*, is perform'd two ways, either by *fpringing* and *falling* on the fame Foot which moves forward, which I fhall, for the future, call a *Bound* ; or *fpringing* and *falling* on the Foot that does not move forward, which I fhall call a *Hop*.

When there is a Mark of a *Spring* upon the *Step*, and no Mark for the holding up of the Foot after it, it fhews, that the *Spring* is to be made with the *Foot* that moves, which is call'd a *Bound*.

A Bound.

A Bound.

But when there is a Mark for a *Spring*, and afterwards a Mark for the *Foot* up, it fignifies, that the *Spring* muft be made on the *Foot* that does not move afterwards, which is call'd a *Hop*. *Forwards*

A Hop.

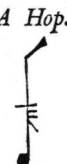

The mark for *falling*, has no proper Place affign'd it, and I fhall only obferve, that in *rifing*, when it is in Order to *fall*, it is neceffary the Mark for a *Rife*, fhould be near the beginning of the *Step*.

Rife and Fall.

The mark for a *Slide*, has likewife no proper Place, when it is fingle on a *Step*; but when it is accompanied with other Marks, as *finking*, *rifing*, &c. then it muft be plac'd laft.

Sink, Rife, and Slide.

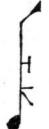

D   If

If after the Mark of a *Slide*, there be alſo the Mark for the Foot up, you muſt *Slide* no farther than that Mark ſhewing the Foot up. *Slide, and afterwards hold the Foot up.*

The Mark for the *Foot up*, may be plac'd either in the Middle, or the End ; when it is in the Middle, it ſhews, that the *Foot* is only up, in Order to be ſet down afterwards.

Foot up, and then put down.

But when it is at the End, it ſignifies, that the Foot muſt remain up. *Foot up.*

'To *point the Toe,* and afterwards the *Heel,* there muſt be a Point on the outſide of that which repreſents the *Toe,* and another on the inſide of that which repreſents the *Heel.*

To point the Toe, and after to place the Heel.

'To *place the Heel,* and afterwards *point the Toe,* there muſt be a point on the outſide of that which repreſents the *Heel,* and another on the inſide of that which repreſents the *Toe.*

It

To place the Heel, and afterwards point the Toe.

It is to be obſerved, that in the two foregoing Examples, the Point which is on the Outſide of that which repreſents either the *Toe* or *Heel,* is the Point from whence you muſt always begin.

When there is a Point at the end of that which repreſents. the *Toe,* and another behind that which ſhews the *Heel,* it ſhews, that the *Foot* muſt be ſet down *flat.*

A flat Foot.

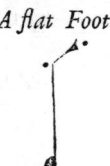

Marks for *Turning,* have no proper Places aſſign'd them, no more than the *falling* or *ſliding* Mark ; but you muſt then obſerve to which ſide to turn, whether to the right or left.

You muſt obſerve, that the beginning of the *turning* Mark, is to be taken from that Part which is neareſt to the black Spot.

After having thus ſhewn the beginning of each *turning Mark,* you muſt obſerve exactly which way to turn, whether to the *right* or *left,* as appears by the following Examples :

A quarter Turn to the Right.	A quarter Turn to the Left.	A half Turn to the Right.	A half Turn to the Left.	Three qua. Turn to the Right.	Three qu. Turn to the Left.

Th

The beginning of a *whole Turn,* or *turn quite round,* is more difficult to find out, becaufe the *Circle,* which is the Mark of it, has neither beginning nor End : But it is neverthelefs to be known by a *Point* plac'd on the fide of the *Step* ; from which *Point* the beginning being known, you make Ufe of the fame Rules as above.

A whole Turn to the Right.   *A whole Turn to the Left.*

When a *Turn* is to be made but half a quarter round, it muft be mark'd a quarter of a *Circle* on the fide of the *Step,* without joining it to the *Step.*

A half quarter Turn to the Left.   *A half quarter Turn to the Right.*

I have already fhewn, that all *Steps* and half *Pofitions,* which have but one Point at either of their Extremities, fignify either the pointing of the *Toe,* or placing the *Heel,* without the Body's bearing on it ; but when there happens to be two Points, it then fhews, that the Body muft bear upon it.

To bear the Body on the Toe.   *To bear the Body on the Heel.*

Having explain'd all the before-mention'd *Marks,* I hope it will not be thought improper to fhew when *Sinkings, Rifings, Spring-*
ings,

ings, and *Slidings,* are to be made upon the *Toe, Heel,* or *flat Foot,* as the following Examples will demonftrate.

When there is a Point at the end of the *finking* Mark, it fhews, that the *Toe* muft be bent downwards.

Sink, the Toe towards the Ground.

When there is a Point behind the *finking* Mark, it denotes, that the *Heel* muft be bent downwards.

Sink, the Heel towards the Ground.

When there is a Point at the end of the *finking* Mark, and a-nother behind, it fhews the *Sink* muft be with a *flat Foot.*

Sink, the Foot flat.

When there is a Point at the end of a *rifing* Mark, it fhews the *Rife* muft be made on the *Toe.*

Rife on the Toe.

When

When there is a Point behind the *rifing* Mark, it fhews, that the *Rife* muft be made on the *Heel.*

Rife on the Heel.

When there is a Point at the end of a *rifing* Mark, and another behind, it fhews, that the *Rife* muft be on a *flat Foot.*

Rife on a flat Foot.

When there is a Point at the end of a *fpringing* Mark, it fhews, that the *Spring, Hop,* or *Bound,* muft be made on the *Toe.*

Spring on the Toe.

When there is a Point behind the *fpringing* Mark, it fhews, that the *Spring, Hop,* or *Bound,* muft be made on the *Heel.*

Spring on the Heel.

When there is a Point at the end of the *fpringing* Mark, and another behind, it fignifies, that the *Spring, Hop,* or *Bound,* muft be made on a *flat Foot.*

Spring

Spring on a flat Foot.

When there is a Point at the end of the *ſliding* Mark, towards the Mark repreſenting the Foot, it ſhews, that the *Slide* muſt be made on the Toe.

Slide on the Toe.

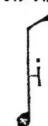

When there is a Point at the other end of the *ſliding* Mark, it ſhews, that the *Slide* is to be made on the Heel.

Slide on the Heel.

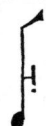

And when there is a Point at each end of the *ſliding* Mark, it denotes, that the *Slide* muſt be made with a flat Foot.

Slide with a flat Foot.

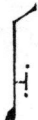

Of marking the Poſitions.

ALL the *Marks* which have been hitherto demonſtrated, may be plac'd as well upon the *half Poſitions* or *Poſitions*, as up-on the *Steps*, the *ſliding* Marks only excepted.   If

The Art of Dancing.

If there were, for Example, a *finking Mark* upon a *half Pofiti-on*, it would fhew, that the Knee of that Leg only was to be bent ; but if *finking Marks* fhould be on the *whole Pofition*, then both Knees are to be *bent* at the fame time. The fame is to be obferv'd for *Rifing, Springing, &c.* The *Marks* on the *Pofitions*, have no appointed Place, as they have on *Steps*, excepting *Points*, which are to be plac'd in the fame manner as on *Steps*.

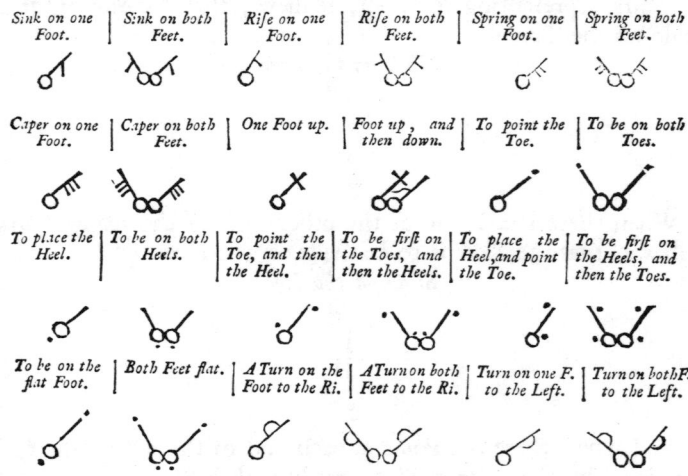

Sink on one Foot.	Sink on both Feet.	Rife on one Foot.	Rife on both Feet.	Spring on one Foot.	Spring on both Feet.

Caper on one Foot.	Caper on both Feet.	One Foot up.	Foot up , and then down.	To point the Toe.	To be on both Toes.

To place the Heel.	To be on both Heels.	To point the Toe, and then the Heel.	To be first on the Toes, and then the Heels.	To place the Heel, and point the Toe.	To be first on the Heels, and then the Toes.

To be on the flat Foot.	Both Feet flat.	A Turn on the Foot to the Ri.	A Turn on both Feet to the Ri.	Turn on one F. to the Left.	Turn on both F. to the Left.

Of Pofitions *and* half Pofitions *having feveral Marks at once.*

POfitions and *half Pofitions* may have feveral *Marks* together, as *Steps* have ; and it muft be obferv'd of the *Marks* for *Sinking, Rifing, Springing*, and *Capers*, that the *Mark* plac'd neareft to the o, is what muft be firft made ; but when there is the *Mark* for the Foot up, that muft certainly be the laft perform'd.

Sink.

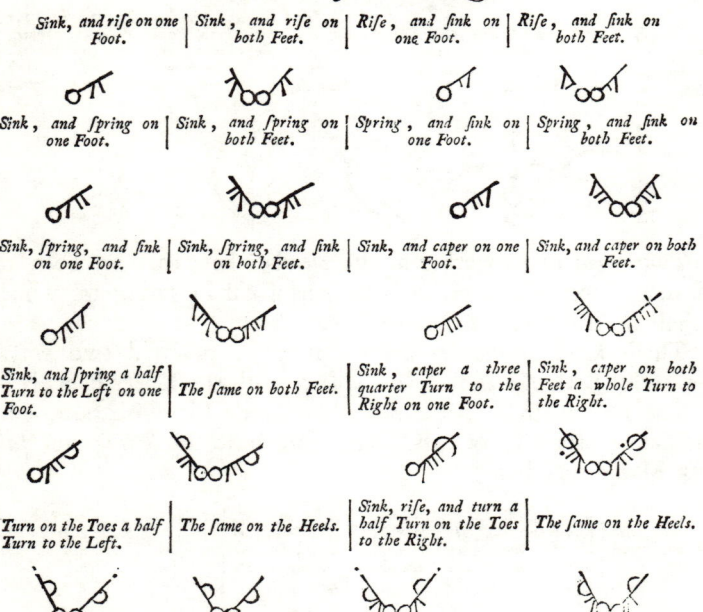

| Sink, and rise on one Foot. | Sink, and rise on both Feet. | Rise, and sink on one Foot. | Rise, and sink on both Feet. |

| Sink, and spring on one Foot. | Sink, and spring on both Feet. | Spring, and sink on one Foot. | Spring, and sink on both Feet. |

| Sink, spring, and sink on one Foot. | Sink, spring, and sink on both Feet. | Sink, and caper on one Foot. | Sink, and caper on both Feet. |

| Sink, and spring a half Turn to the Left on one Foot. | The same on both Feet. | Sink, caper a three quarter Turn to the Right on one Foot. | Sink, caper on both Feet a whole Turn to the Right. |

| Turn on the Toes a half Turn to the Left. | The same on the Heels. | Sink, rise, and turn a half Turn on the Toes to the Right. | The same on the Heels. |

All the Marks of *sinking* and *rising*, which have been already demonstrated upon the *Step*, have Relation to the *Bendings* and *Risings* of both the Knees : But when it shall happen, that in moving in a Dance, one *Knee* only ought to *bend* or *rise*, the following Rules must be observed.

It will be necessary upon this Occasion, to understand when one Leg moves, what the other ought to do ; to demonstrate which, I shall make use of a *half Position* and a *Step*, which must be ty'd together by a small Line, of which, one end is join'd to that which represents the *Heel* of the *half Position*, and the other to the Head of the *Step*. This Union denotes, that the *half Position* and the *Step*, are both to act at the same time.

E

To

To bend the left Knee, while the right moves extended.	To bend, and rise the left Knee, while the right moves extended.	To bend the left Knee, moving the right half way extended, and afterwards to bend in moving.	To bend the left Knee, the right moving extended, and sink in the middle of the Step, and rise on the Toes.	To bend the right Knee in moving, and rise towards the left continuing extended.

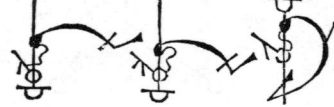  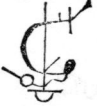

    Two *Steps* ty'd together at the Heads, shew they are both to move at once, which can only be perform'd by *springing*, which I shall hereafter call a *starting Step*.

    These kind of *starting Steps*, may be practis'd two ways, *viz.* with both *Knees* stiff, or falling with the Knees bent.

    The first of these needs no other Mark for Direction, but the *sliding Mark*; but the other must have the *sliding* and *falling* Marks together.

To spring with both Feet open at once.	With one Foot forwards, and the other backwards, both at once.	A starting Step, with both Feet open, the Knees stiff.	A starting Step, one Foot forwards, the other backwards, the Knees stiff.	A starting Step, with both Feet open, and falling with both Knees bent.	The same, one Foot backwards, the other forwards.

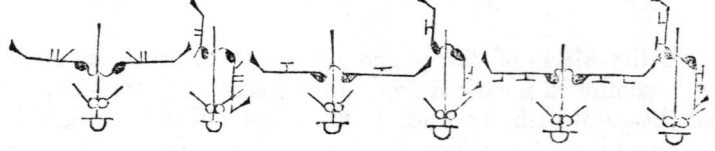

Of waving Positions, and half Positions.

A *Waving Position*, or half *Position*, is when the Foot *waves* or *turns* inwards or outwards, whether upon the *Toe*, the Heel, or with the *Foot* up, which is explain'd by a kind of *Half-Moon* proceeding from that place which reprefents either the Heel or *Toe*, and which demonstrates the Motion the Heel or

Toe

Toe ought to make in *Waving*. If it be to wave upon the *Toe*, the *Crefcent* or *Half-Moon* ought to be plac'd where the *Heel* is reprefented, tending towards the *Toes* on that fide you are to wave; on the contrary, if the *waving Step* is to be done on the *Heel*, or with the Foot up, the *Crefcent* muft be in the place which reprefents the *Toes* tending towards the *Heel*.

Waving on the Toe, the Heel opening outwards.	*The fame on both Toes.*	*Waving on the Heel, the Toe clofing inwards.*	*The fame on both Heels.*	*Waving with the Foot up, the Toe clofing inwards.*

Of Pofitions and half Pofitions, which are wav'd and unwav'd.

POfitions and half *Pofitions*, *wav'd* and *unwav'd*, are when the *Heel* or *Toe* returns to the place from whence either of them mov'd, which is explain'd by the *Crefcent* being doubled, returning to the place from whence it came.

Waving and un-waving, the Heel opening outwards, and then clofing inwards.	*The fame with both Feet.*	*Waving and unwaving, the Toe clofing inwards, and afterwards opening outwards.*	*The fame with both Feet.*	*Waving and unwaving with the Foot up, the Toe clofing inwards, and then opening outwards.*

Examples of waving Pofitions, where the *Toes* or *Heels* wave both one way, and are diftinguifh'd by the *Crefcents* being both on the fame fide.

Waving

| Waving on both Toes, the Heels moving to the Right. | The same to the Left. | Waving on both Heels, the Toes moving to the Left. | The same to the Right. |

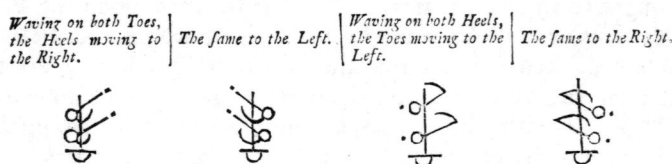

Examples of waving and unwaving Positions, where the Feet turn and return both on the same side.

| To turn on the Toes, the two Heels moving to the Right, and returning to the Left. | The same to the Left, and to the Right. | To turn on the two Heels, the Toes moving to the Left, and then returning to the Right. | The same to the Right, and to the Left. |

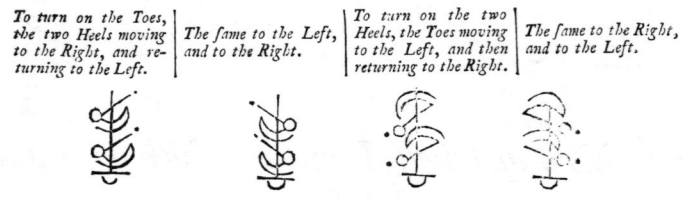

Of the Change of Positions.

THE *Change* of *Positions*, is *changing* or *shifting* from one *Position* to another, whether true or false; to wit, from the first to the second, from the second to the third, and so on.

The Change of Positions is made two ways, either by *springing*, or *waving*.

Those which are perform'd by *springing*, are done when you *spring* from one Position, and fall in another; and those which are perform'd by waving, must be done on the Ground, by waving the two Feet, or each Foot separately, either on the Toes or Heels.

The shifting of *Positions* by *springing*, may be known by what follows, *viz.* by two *Positions*, one of which has *springing* on it, and the other none.

A

a TABLE of ỹ shifting of ỹ True Positions		a TABLE of ỹ Changing of ỹ False Positions	
from ỹ 1st. to ỹ 2d.	from ỹ 1st to ỹ 3d.	from ỹ 1st to ỹ 2d.	from ỹ 1st to ỹ 3d.
from ỹ 1st to ỹ 4th.	from ỹ 1st to ỹ 5th	from ỹ 1st to ỹ 4th	from ỹ 1st to ỹ 5th
from ỹ 2d. to ỹ 3d.	from ỹ 3d. to ỹ 5th.	from ỹ 2d to ỹ 3d.	from ỹ 3d to ỹ 1st.
from ỹ 4th. to ỹ 2d.	from ỹ 5th. to ỹ 1st.	from ỹ 4th to ỹ 2d.	from ỹ 5th to ỹ 4th
from ỹ 4th to ỹ 4th.	from ỹ 3d to ỹ 3d.	from ỹ 3d to ỹ 3d.	from ỹ 4th to ỹ 4th.

a **TABLE** of ỹ Changing true positions into false positions		a **TABLE** of shifting from false positions to true ones.	
from ỹ 1.st true to ỹ 2.d false.	from ỹ 1.st true to ỹ 3.d false.	from ỹ 1.st false to ỹ 2.d true.	from ỹ 1.st false to ỹ 3.d true
from ỹ 1.st true to ỹ 4.th false.	from ỹ 1.st true to ỹ 5.th false.	from ỹ 1.st false to ỹ 4.th true.	from ỹ 1.st false to ỹ 5.th true.
from ỹ 2.d true to ỹ 3.d false.	from ỹ 3.d true to ỹ 1.st false.	from ỹ 2.d false to ỹ 3.d true.	from ỹ 3.d false to ỹ 4.th true.
from ỹ 4.th true to ỹ 5.th false.	from ỹ 5.th true to ỹ 2.d false.	from ỹ 4.th false to ỹ 1.st true.	from ỹ 5.th false to ỹ 2.d true.
from ỹ 1.st true to ỹ 1.st false.	from ỹ 3.d true to ỹ 3.d false.	from ỹ 2.d false to ỹ 2.d true.	from ỹ 3.d false to ỹ 3.d true.
	&c		

The *Pofition* which has *fpringing* Marks on it, fhews from whence the *Spring* is to be made, and that which has no *fpringing* Marks on it, only denotes in what *Pofition* to fall, as may be feen by the foregoing Tables.

Of Pofitions that fhift or change from one place to another.

POfitions may alfo change in *fpringing* from one place to another, as in *fpringing* forwards, backwards, or fideways. This is explain'd by two Lines of Communication, that go from the *Pofition* on which the *fpringing Marks* are plac'd, to that where there are none : Which Lines denote the Extenfion of the *Spring,* and of which fide it muft fall.

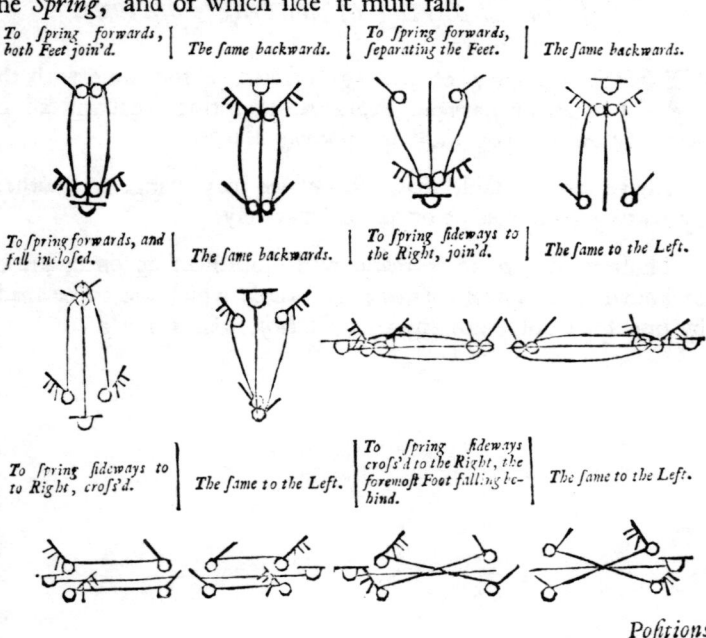

To fpring forwards, | both Feet join'd. | The fame backwards. | To fpring forwards, | feparating the Feet. | The fame backwards.

To fpring forwards, and | fall inclofed. | The fame backwards. | To fpring fideways to | the Right, join'd. | The fame to the Left.

To fpring fideways to | to Right, crofs'd. | The fame to the Left. | To fpring fideways | crofs'd to the Right, the | foremoft Foot falling be- | hind. | The fame to the Left.

Pofitions may alfo change in *fpringing*, by two *Steps* being ty'd together at the Heads ; which fhews, that they muft move both at the fame time.

A Spring forwards, with both Feet join'd. | The fame backwards. | To fpring from the firft Pofition to the fecond. | To fpring from the fe- cond to the firft.

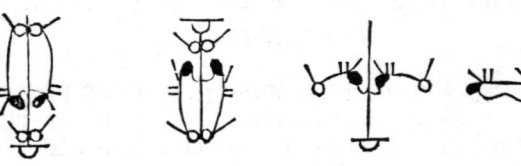

Of the Changing of waving Pofitions.

THE Changing of *waving Pofitions*, is the fame with the Change of *fpringing Pofitions*, excepting, that inftead of *fpringing Marks*, you muft ufe *waving Marks*.

I have already faid, that one *Pofition* may change to another, by *waving* both Feet at once, or feparately.

Thofe which are to be made with both Feet at once, are to be known by a *wav'd Pofition* ; and thofe which are to be made by one Foot only, are known by a *half Pofition wav'd*.

The Changing of Waving Positions			
from y̌ 1st true to y̌ 2d false	*from y̌ 2d false to y̌ 1st true*	*from y̌ 1st false to y̌ 2d true*	*from y̌ 2d true to y̌ 1st false*
from y̌ 3d true to y̌ 2d false.	*from y̌ 2d false to y̌ 3d true*	*from y̌ 3d true to y̌ 3d false*	*from y̌ 3d false to y̌ 2d true*
from y̌ 2d true to y̌ 3d false.	*from y̌ 3 false to y̌ 3d true*	*from y̌ 3d false to y̌ 3d false*	*from y̌ 3d false to y̌ 3 false*
from y̌ 5th true to y̌ 4th false	*from y̌ 4th false to y̌ 5th true*	*from y̌ 1st true to y̌ 1st false*	*from y̌ 1st false to y̌ 1st true*

How to hold the Book or Paper, to decipher written Dances.

YOU muſt underſtand, that each Page, on which the *Dance* is deſcribed, repreſents the *Dancing-Room*; and the four
Sides

as EF do the upper end of the Room, G H
^ The lower part.

Sides of the Page, the four Sides of the *Room*, viz. the upper part
of the Page, reprefents the upper end of the *Room* ; the lower
part, the lower end ; the right fide of the Page, the right fide
of the *Room* ; and the left fide, the left, as you may fee by the
following Figure, of which A B C D reprefent the *Room*, and
E F G H, the Page. E F fhew the upper part of the Page, as
C D do the lower end ; F H the right fide of the Page, as B
D the right fide of the *Room* ; and E G the left fide of the Page,
as A C the left fide of the *Room*.

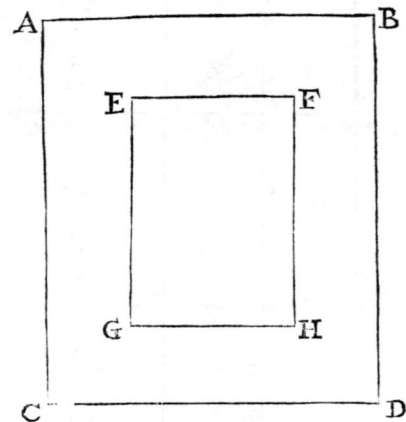

You muft obferve always to hold the upper end of the Book
againft the upper end of the *Room*; and whether the *Dance* have
any *Turning* in it or not, you muft carefully avoid removing the
Book from the Scituation above demonftrated.

When any *Steps* are made without *turning*, or in *turning* quite
round, then both fides of the Book muft be held with both
Hands; but in *turning* a quarter round, half round, or three
quarters round, it will be neceffary to take more Care, becaufe

                                                              it

it will be difficult to *turn*, unlefs the Book turns alfo ; yet this muft be abfolutely avoided ; for if the Book moves out of its Scituation, it will be impoffible to comprehend the *Steps* therein defcrib'd ; wherefore, for the better Obfervation of this, I fhall give you the following Rules.

After having confider'd the *Turning*, and on what fide to turn, as for Example, in a quarter *Turn* to the Right, you muft put your left Hand to the farther part of the Book, and your Right to the neareft. Your Hands being thus prepared, in turning your quarter *Turn*, bring your left Hand in to you, whilft your right removes from you ; fo that both Hands will by this means be equally advanc'd before you, holding the Book by the fame places before-mention'd, and you will find, that in turning a quarter round, the Book will ftill remain in its former Scituation. You muft make ufe of the fame Rule in a *half Turn*.

I fhall only add, that the Hand, which is plac'd on the moft oppofite part of the Book, muft come quite in to your Breaft, while the other removes quite from you.

To turn *three quarters round* to the Right, you muft crofs your Hands more than you did in the *half Turn* ; fo that your left Hand muft hold the upper part of that fide which your right Hand would naturally have held, had you not turn'd ; and your right Hand muft hold the lower part of that fide, which your left would otherwife have held. Your Hands being thus prepar'd, you will turn *three quarters round* in the fame manner as you did *half round*.

The fame Rules may be made ufe of in *turning* to the left, only you muft obferve, that inftead of placing your left Hand, you muft place the right to that part of the Book the fartheft from you ; and it may ferve for a general Rule, that in turning to the Right, you firft remove your left Hand ; and in turning to the Left, you remove your Right.

F

Rules to be obferv'd in Dancing by written Cha-racters.

YOU muft firft find out the beginning of the *Tract*, by which means you will know towards what part of the *Dancing-Room* the Body is to be plac'd, before the *Dance* begins, as has been fhewn before, in fpeaking of the *Pofture*, and *Prefence of the Body.* Then obferve whether there be any *Pofition*, as you will find in the following Examples, and there you are to place your felf. Then fee what *Step* is nearest to the faid *Pofition*, and you will find it to be that which is mark'd *Number* 1. Which having perform'd, obferve which is nearest to that, and you will find it is that mark'd *Number* 2. After this, you muft move to *Number* 3, then to *Number* 4, *&c.* and fo continue moving, obferving exactly to perform that *Step* which is nearest to the place where you are, and to follow always the fame *Rule* as well in moving forwards, backwards, and fideways, as in moving round.

Examples.

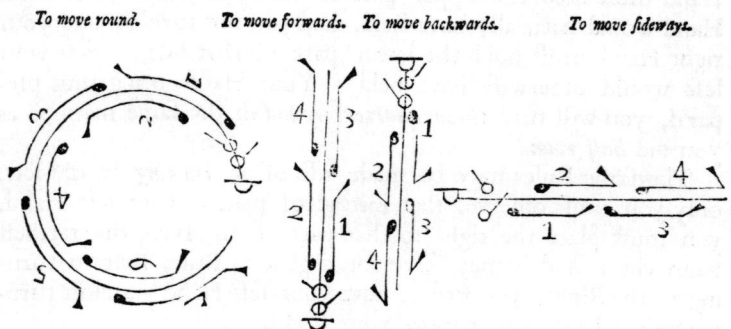

To move round.　　To move forwards.　To move backwards.　　To move fideways.

How to know what Steps *and* half Pofitions *are with the right Foot, and what with the left.*

THE *Tract* or *Line*, on which *Dances* are defcrib'd, whether forward or backward, muft be confider'd in refpect
to its right fide mark'd R, and the left fide mark'd L, as may
be feen by the following *Example.*

The *Steps* and *half Pofitions*, which are on the right fide, are
made with the right Foot ; and thofe which are on the left fide,
with the left Foot, as the following *Movements* will demonftrate,
where I fhall give to each *Step* and *half Pofition*, the fame Letters
r and l, the better to explain them.

Befides the Letters, r and l, the *Steps* and *half Pofitions* of the
right or left Foot, will be eafily known, by obferving which
way the *Toes* are turn'd.

The *Toe* turning outwards on the right fide, is the right Foot,
and the *Toe* turning outwards on the left fide, is the left.

The different *Tracts* or *Figures* made in *Dancing*, whether forwards, backwards, fideways, or round, will be explain'd by what
follows.

The *Tract* mark'd A, is moving forwards, the Face towards
the upper end of the *Room.*

The *Tract* B retires or goes back, the Face towards the lower
end of the *Room.*

The *Tract* F is moving forwards, the Face towards the right
fide of the *Room.*

The *Tract* H retires, the Face towards the left fide of the *Room.*

The *Tract* I, moves forwards, the Face towards the left fide
of the *Room.*

· The *Tract* K retires backwards, the Face towards the right fide
of the *Room.*

The *Tracts* G, move round, and the *Tracts* M, retire round.

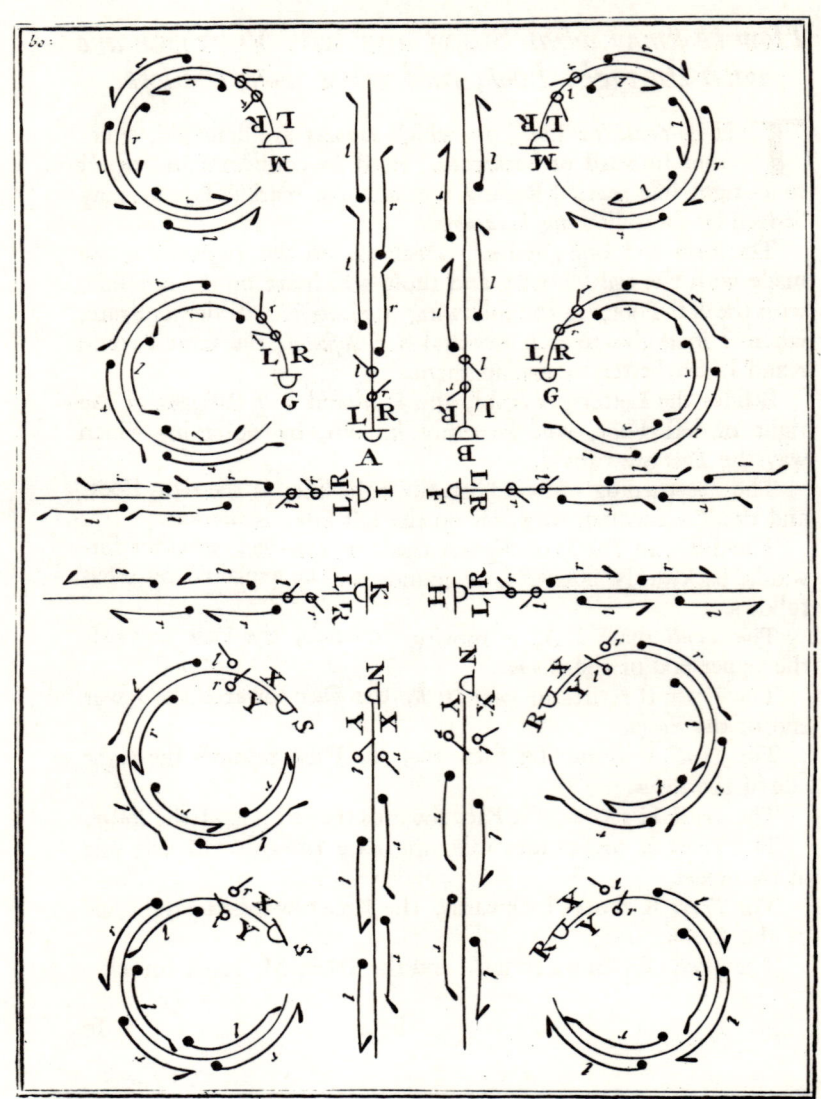

In moving fideways, the *Tract* or *Line* muft alfo be confidered as to its two fides, *viz.* the upper fide mark'd X, and the under fide mark'd Y. *Steps* and *half Pofitions,* which are on the upper fide of the Line, are to be made with the foremoft Foot, and thofe which are on the under fide, with the hinder Foot.

The *Tracts* mark'd N, are moving fideways to the right, towards the lower end of the *Room.*

The *Tracts* R, move round fideways to the right.

And the *Tracts* S, move round fideways to the left.

The manner of Steps croffing one another.

A *Step* which begins with the hind Foot, in order to move fideways, to end on a Line with the other Foot, ought to begin from the part under the Line, and rife obliquely fideways towards that above, as you may fee by the following *Step.*

To move the right Foot fideways.   *To move the left Foot fideways.*

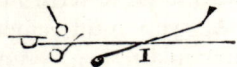   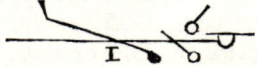

A *Step,* which is to crofs behind the foregoing *Step,* muft begin above the Line, and defcend obliquely below it ; and which you will eafily underftand by the following Example : The firft *Step* you may know by *Number* 1, and the other, which croffes, by *Number* 2.

To move the right Foot fideways, and crofs the left behind.   *To move the left Foot fideways, and crofs the right behind.*

A *Step,* which begins with the foremoft Foot, in order to move fideways, to end on a Line with the other Foot, ought to begin from the part above the Line, and defcend obliquely fideways towards that below, as the following *Step,* mark'd *Number* 1, will fhew.

To

To move the right Foot sideways.   *To move the left Foot sideways.*

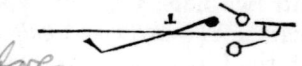

A *Step*, which is to crofs behind the foregoing *Step*, muft begin from below the Line, and rife obliquely above it, which you may obferve by the *Step Number* 1.

To move the right Foot sideways, and crofs the left before.   *To move the left Foot sideways, and crofs the right before.*

To return upon a Tract you have juft before mov'd on.

FOR *Example*, if you have mov'd from the lower end of the *Room*, to the upper end, and have a mind to return upon the fame *Tract*, as the *Tract* mark'd A, you muft remove, and place the *Line* or *Tract*, on which you would return, on one fide or the other, as you fhall find moft convenient, as is mark'd by the Letter B, and which in effect is the fame with the foregoing ; which two *Tracts* muft be join'd together by a pointed *Line* mark'd C, which only ferves to conduct the Sight from one *Line* to the other.

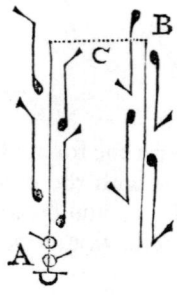

The

The fame thing muft be obferv'd in moving feveral times round on the fame *Circle*, as upon the *Circle* mark'd D ; about which may be defcrib'd as many *Circles* as fhall be neceffary. As for *Example*, the *Circles* E and F, which muft be fuppofed to be on the fame *Circle* with the *Circle* D.

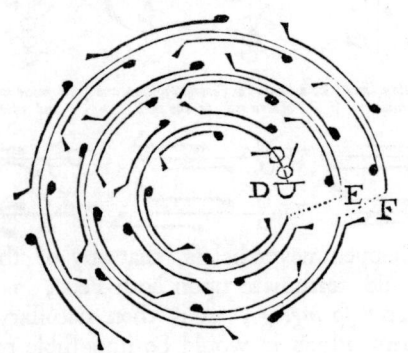

To know to and from what Pofitions, Steps move.

I Might have mark'd the *Pofitions*, in which each *Step* ought to terminate ; but fince this muft have created a great deal of Trouble, I fhall only confine my felf to mark them on join'd and inclos'd *Steps*, and for the reft, whether forwards, backwards, fideways, or crofs'd, the *Pofitions* may be eafily known, without marking them, in obferving that which follows.

Steps which move forwards or backwards, fhall be taken to be in the fourth *Pofition*.

Steps which move ftreight, opening fideways, fhall be taken to be in fecond the *Pofition*, and *Steps* croffing, whether forwards or backwards, fhall be taken to be in the fifth *Pofition*.

| To move to the fourth Position, and afterwards to the second. | To move to the fifth Position, and afterwards to the second. | To move to the fifth Position, and afterwards to the fourth. |

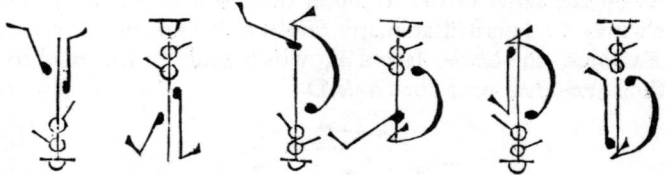

| To move to the fifth Position, and afterwards to the second. | To move to the second Position, and afterwards to the fifth. | To move to the second Position, and afterwards to the fifth. |

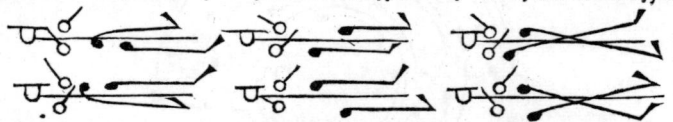

If it should happen nevertheless, that any of the above-mention'd *Steps* should terminate upon both Feet, as it often happens in *rising* and *springing*, it is then necessary to mark the *Position*; without which it would be impossible to know, that the *rising* and *springing* should be on both Feet; wherefore, in demonstrating the *Positions* of *join'd* and *inclos'd Steps*, I will add to them those before-mention'd, on which I will also mark the *Positions*, to make Use of on Occasion.

How Steps terminate in Positions.

WHEN a *Step* terminates in a *Position*, there ought to be no Foot at the end of it, because the half *Position*, to which it is join'd, serves for that.

| A Step to the first Position forwards. | The same backwards. | A Step to the third Position forwards. | The same backwards. | A Step to the third Position before. | The same behind. |

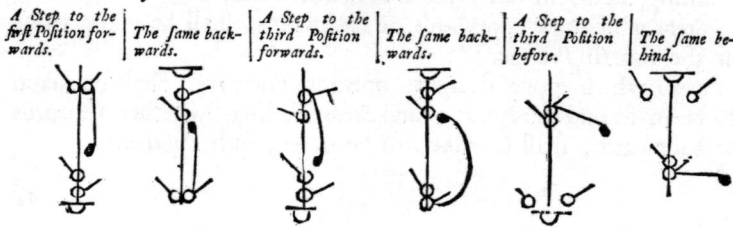

A

A rifing Step on both Feet in the fecond Pofition.	*A Spring on both Feet in the fecond Pofition.*	*A Rife on both Feet in the fourth Pofition.*	*A Spring on both Feet in the fourth Pofition.*	*A Rife on both Feet in the fifth Pofition.*	*A Spring on both Feet in the fifth Pofit.*

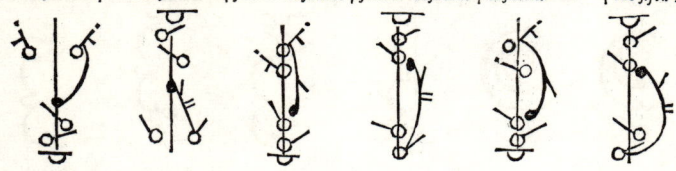

A *Pofition* at the end of a *Step,* may be alfo known by adding to the *Step* a *half Pofition,* becaufe the Reprefentation of the Foot, which is at the Extremity of the *Step,* is made Ufe of, upon this Occafion, for a *half Pofition*; and a *half Pofition* join'd to it, is the fame as a *whole Pofition.*

A join'd Step.	*An inclos'd Step.*

The fame **Rule** muft be obferv'd in *beaten Steps,* viz. That the *half Pofition* reprefents the Foot, againft which the other *beats*; and whereby you may know whether the *Beat* be made on the *Inftep,* behind the Heel, againft the *Ankle,* or againft the fide of the Foot.

A Beat on the Inftep.	*A Beat behind.*	*A Beat on the Inftep, and move behind.*	*A Beat behind and before.*	*A Beat above and below.*	*The fame four times.*

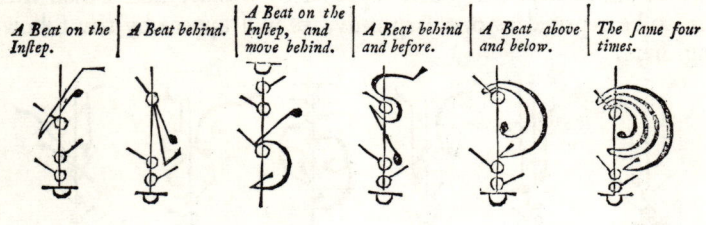

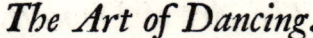

A Beat on the Ankle.	*A Beat 4 times on the Ankle, & behind the Heel.*	*A Beat sideways, moving forwards.*	*The same backwards.*	*The same twice, moving forwards.*	*The same, moving backwards.*

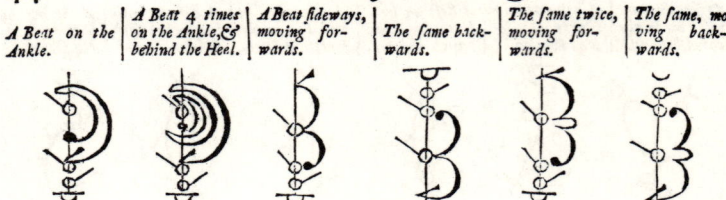

You muſt obſerve, that when two *Steps* terminate bo thin the ſame *Poſition*, the firſt moves without any regard to the *Poſition*, and it is the laſt only that muſt obſerve the ſaid *Poſition*; as the following Examples will demonſtrate.

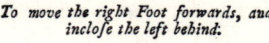

To move the right Foot forwards, and join the left.	*To move the right Foot forwards, and incloſe the left behind.*

Of ſimple and compound Steps.

ALL *Steps* may be either *ſimple* or *compound*.

    A *ſimple Step*, is that which is alone, as all thoſe which have been hitherto demonſtrated; and a *compound Step*, is, where two or more *Steps* are join'd together by a *Line,* and which then are to be reputed as one *Step* only, as will appear by the following *Steps.*

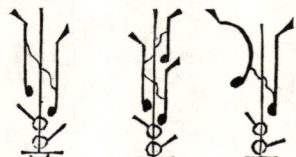
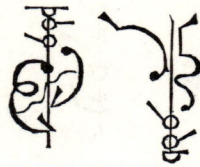

To practife more eafily what has already been taught and demonftrated, you may make Ufe of the following *Tables* ; where you will find all or the greateft Part of the *Steps* us'd in *Dancing*, whether with one Foot, or the other, forwards, backwards, fideways, or turning, as well upon ftreight Lines, as diametrical.

The Tables.

1. Of *Courant Movements*.	8. Of *Siffonne's*, or *Crofs-Leaps*.
2. Of *half Coupee's*.	9. Of *Pirouettes*.
3. Of *Coupee's*.	10. Of *Capers*, and *Half-Capers*.
4. Of *Bouree's*, or *Fleurets*.	11. Of *Entre-chats*, or *Crofs-Capers*.
5. Of *Bounds*, or *Tacs*.	12. Of *Waving Steps*.
6. Of *Contretemps*, or *compos'd Hops*.	13. A *Supplement*.
7. Of *Chaffee's*, or *Drives*.	

You muft obferve, that each Square contains only one *Step*, which I have writ down twice, to the end to fhew, that what is perform'd with one Foot, may alfo be perform'd with the other.

An Explanation of the Steps contain'd in each Square, is alfo writ down with them; and whereas fome of the Words and Terms are abbreviated for want of Room, I have put down here a fhort Explanation of them.

forw.	———— *forwards.*	*circ.*	———— *circular.*
backw.	———— *backwards.*	*jo.*	———— *join'd.*
fidew.	———— *fideways.*	*incl.*	———— *inclos'd.*
fl.	———— *flide.*	*bef.*	———— *before.*
cro.	———— *crofs'd.*	*beh.*	———— *behind.*
op.	———— *open.*	*wav.*	———— *waving.*
qr. Turn	———— *quarter Turn.*	*turn.*	———— *turning.*
bf. Turn	———— *half Turn.*	*outw.*	———— *outwards.*
3 qr. Turn	———— *three quarter Turn.*	*inw.*	———— *inwards.*

Of

TABLES

Conteyning most of the steps us'd in

Dancing

Courant Movements
And Galliard step.

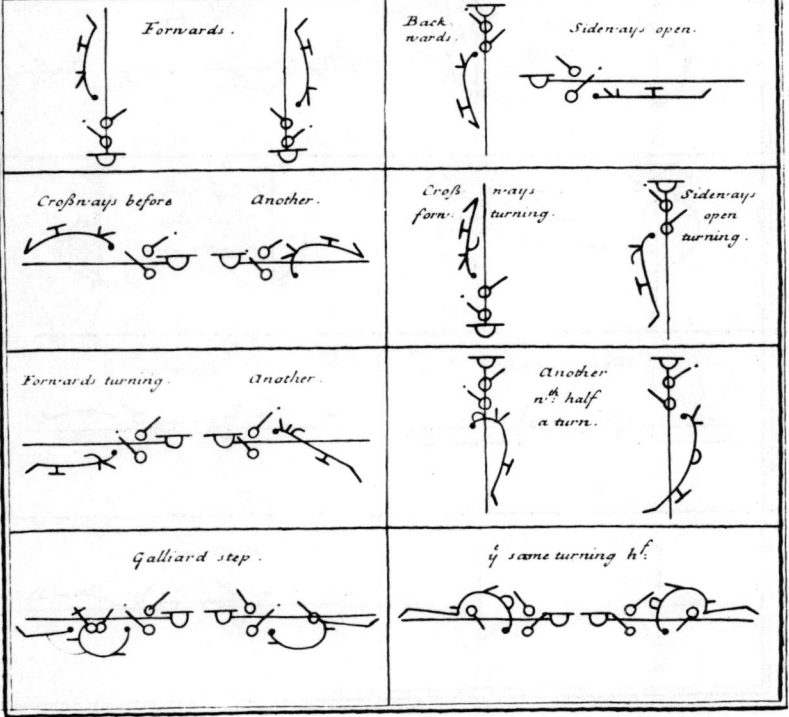

a TABLE *of half Coupees*

Half Coupee forw:	Backwards.
Open backwards.	ẏ same.
ẏ same circular before.	ẏ same circular sideways.
Open sideways.	Another.
Another.	Croßways before.

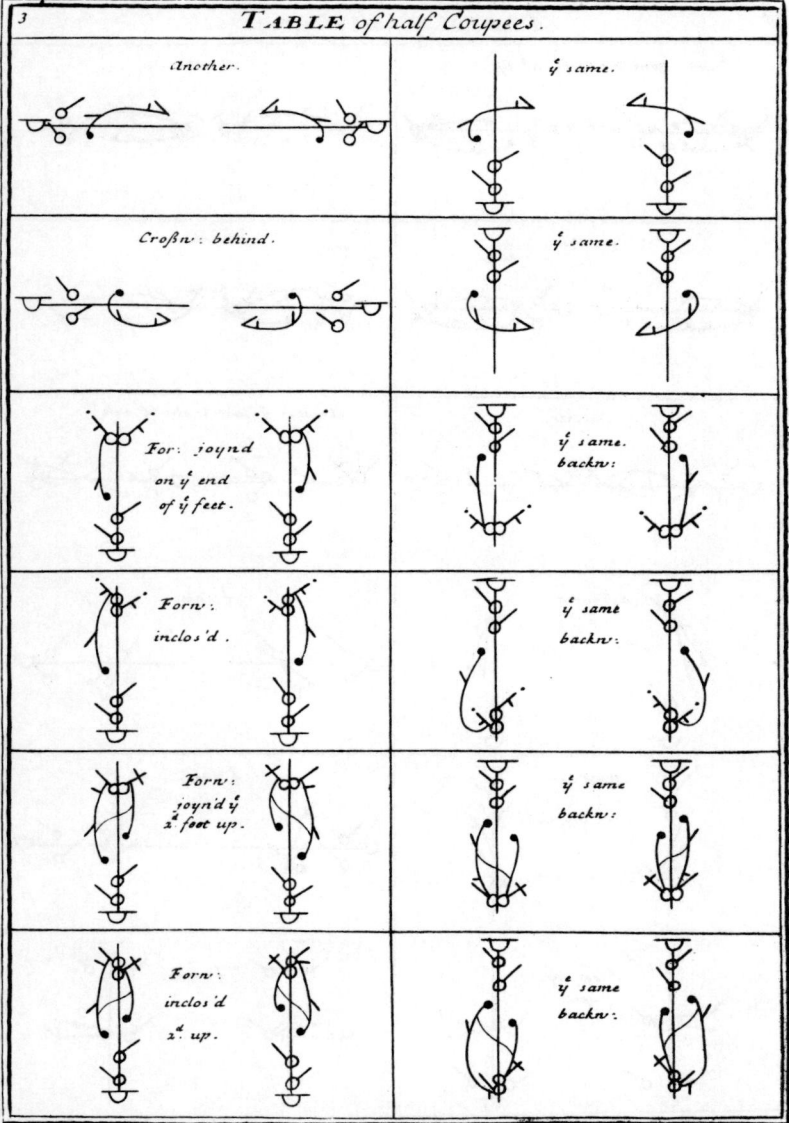

Another.	ỹ same.
Croßn: behind.	ỹ same.
For: joynd on ỹ end of ỹ feet.	ỹ same. backñ:
Forñ: inclos'd.	ỹ same backñ:
Forñ: joyn'd ỹ 2ᵈ foot up.	ỹ same backñ:
Forñ: inclos'd 2ᵈ. up.	ỹ same backñ:

TABLE of half Coupees

Siden: open & joyn'd 2ᵈ up.

Another.

Another.

Another.

Another.

Another ÿ last inclos'd beh:

a Beat beh:

ÿ same.

Beat bef: croſs ÿ ankle.

ÿ same.

Sideways open.

ÿ same.

TABLE of half Coupees

Beat on y͘ ankle open siden

y͘ same.

Croßn͘ forn͘ q͘ turn.

Open sid͘ q͘ turn.

y͘ same.

Another.

Another.

y͘ same.

Forwards turning q͘.

Another.

Another.

Another.

TABLE of half Coupees.

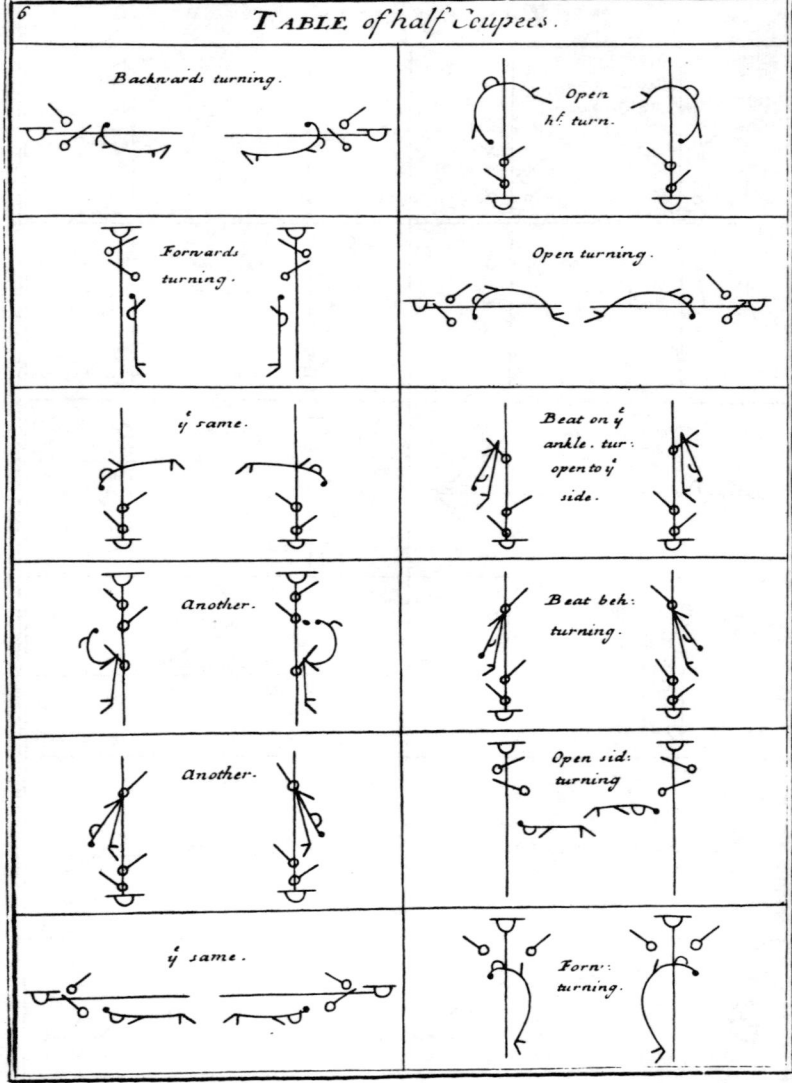

Backwards turning.

Open hf. turn.

Forwards turning.

Open turning.

ý same.

Beat on ý ankle. tur: open to ý side.

Another.

Beat beh: turning.

Another.

Open sid: turning

ý same.

Forn: turning.

TABLE, *of Coupee's*

Coupee forw :	*Backw :*
Forw : 2.d open & up	*Open backw : 2.d open & up.*
Forw : 2.d circular inw : open sidew :	*Op : backw : 2.d circ : & slide forw :*
Forw : 2.d beh : & op : bef : & circular up .	*forw : 2.d beat beh :*
Coupee 2 movements .	*Open back : 2.d beat bef :*

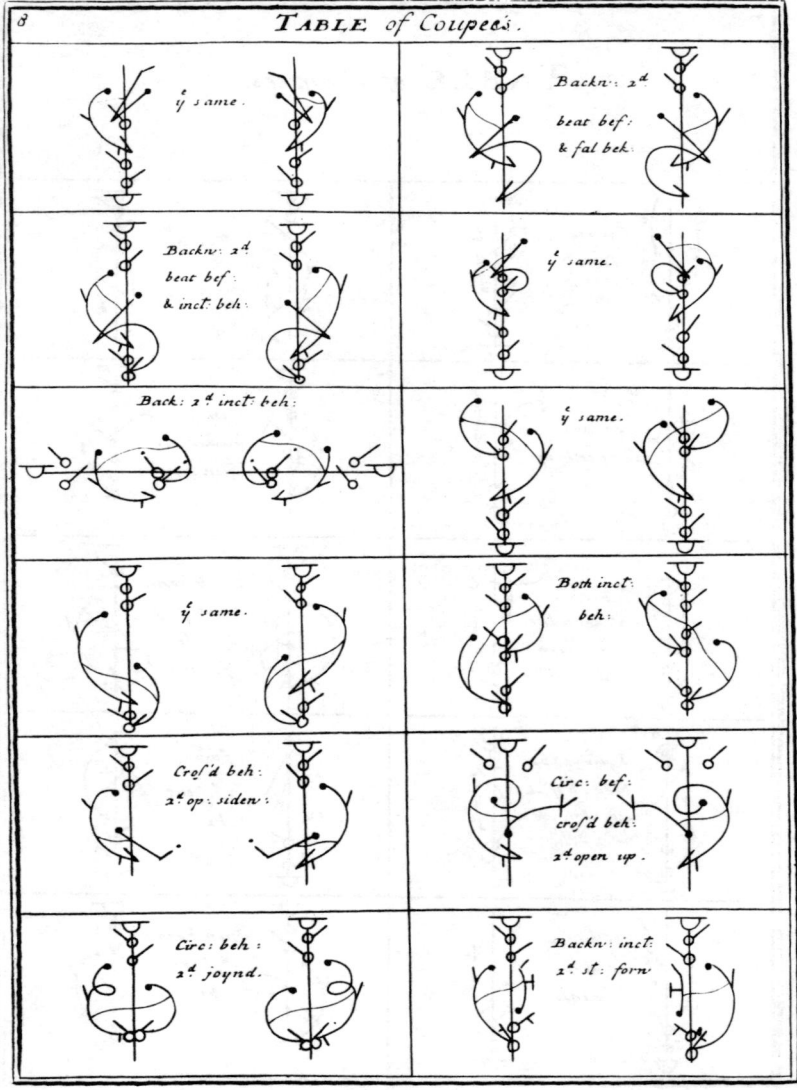

ỹ same.

Backn: 2ᵈ
beat bef:
& fal beh:

Backn: 2ᵈ
beat bef:
& incl: beh:

ỹ same.

Back: 2ᵈ incl: beh:

ỹ same.

ỹ same.

Both incl:
beh:

Crof'd beh:
2ᵈ op: siden:

Circ: bef:
crof'd beh:
2ᵈ open up.

Circ: beh:
2ᵈ joynd.

Backn: incl:
2ᵈ. st: forn:

TABLE of Coupees.

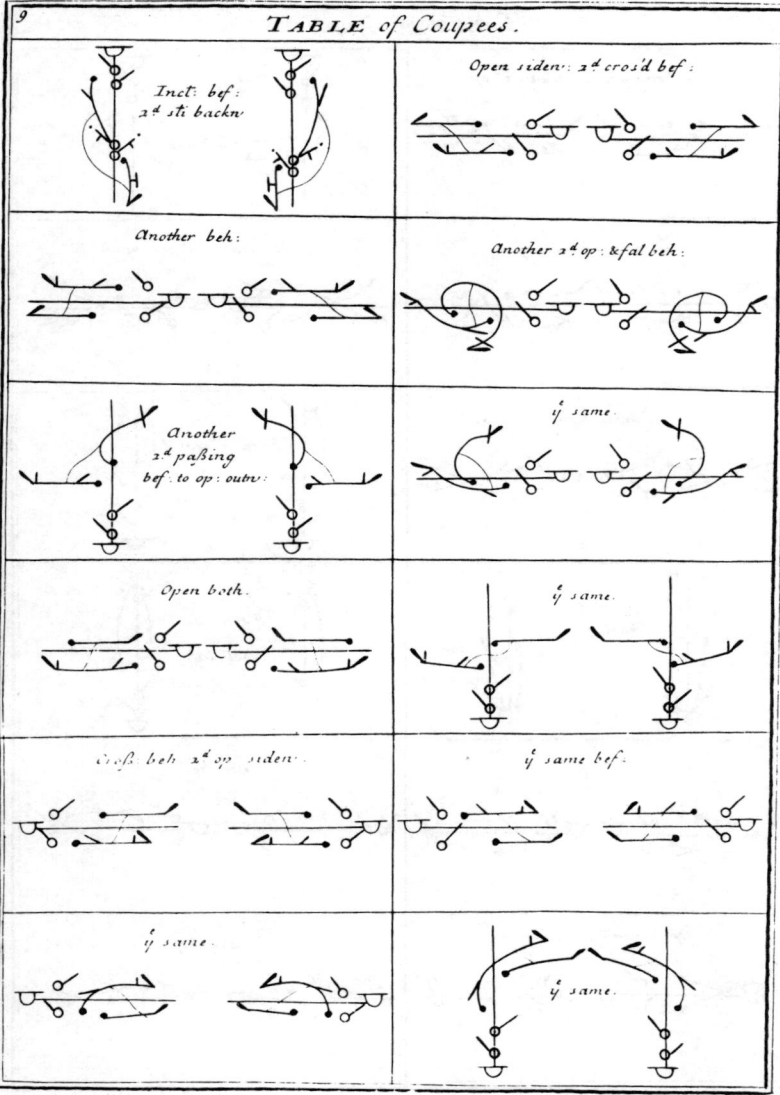

Inct: bef: 2.d sti: backn.

Open siden: 2.d cros'd bef:

Another beh:

Another 2.d op: & fal beh:

Another 2.d paßing bef: to op: outv:

ÿ same.

Open both.

ÿ same.

Croß beh 2.d op siden:

ÿ same bef:

ÿ same.

ÿ same.

TABLE of Coupees.

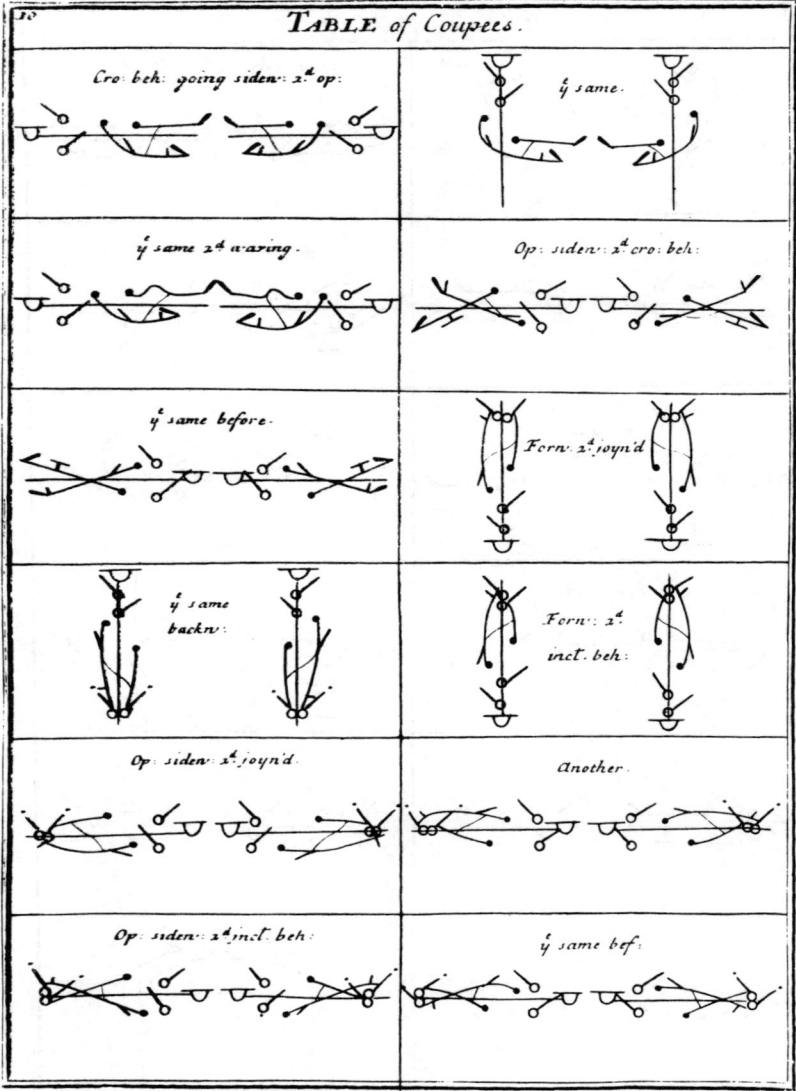

Cro: beh: going siden: 2.ᵈ op:

ý same.

ý same 2ᵈ waving.

Op: siden: 2.ᵈ cro: beh:

ý same before.

Forn: 2.ᵈ joyn'd

ý same backw:

Forn: 2.ᵈ incl. beh:

Op: siden: 2.ᵈ joyn'd.

Another.

Op: siden: 2.ᵈ incl. beh:

ý same bef:

TABLE of Coupees.

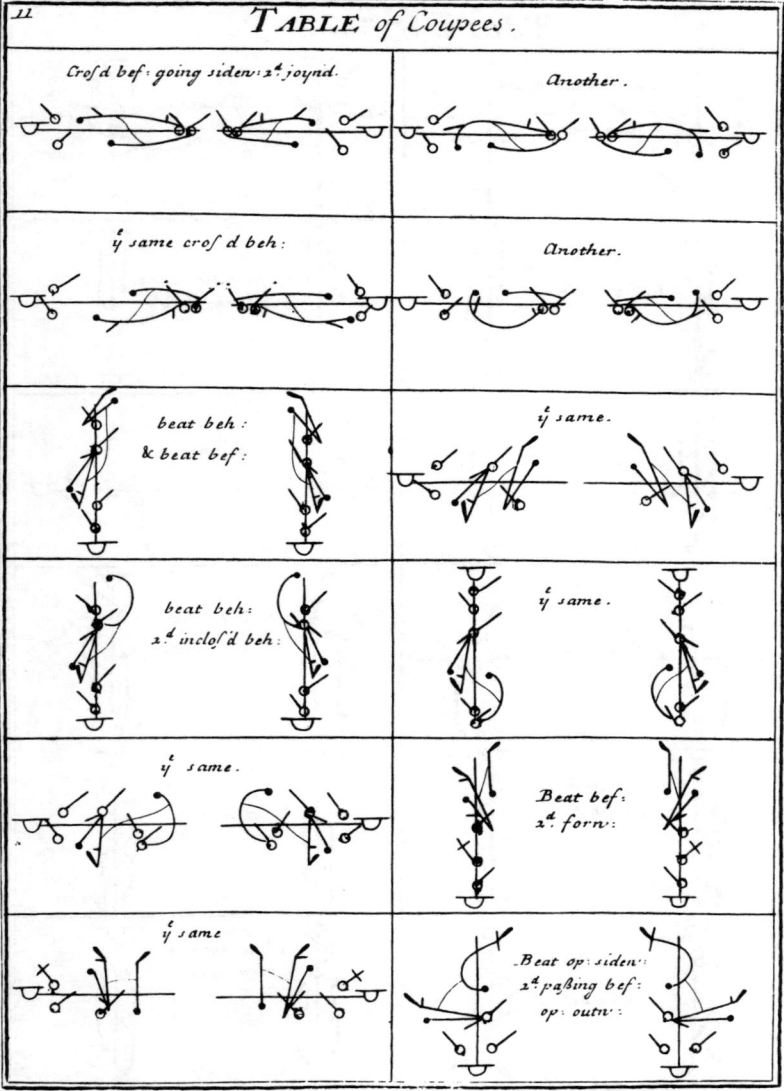

Crost bef: going siden: 2.d joynd.

Another.

ẙ same crosd beh:

Another.

beat beh:
& beat bef:

ẙ same.

beat beh:
2.d inclosd beh:

ẙ same.

ẙ same.

Beat bef:
2.d forn:

ẙ same

Beat op: siden:
2.d paßing bef:
op: outn:

TABLE of Coupees

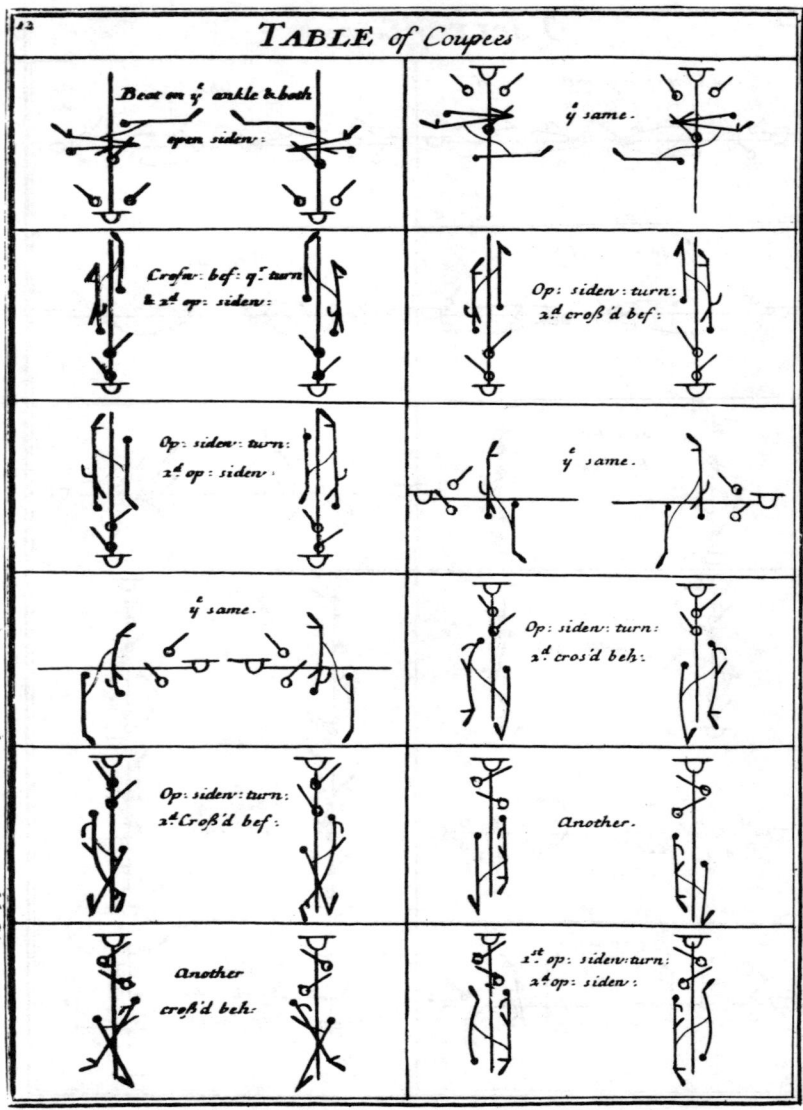

Beat on y⁰ ankle & both open siden :

y⁰ same .

Crofs: bef: q⁰ turn & 2ᵈ op: siden :

Op: siden: turn: 2ᵈ crofs'd bef :

Op: siden: turn: 2ᵈ op: siden ·

y⁰ same .

y⁰ same .

Op: siden: turn: 2ᵈ cros'd beh :

Op: siden: turn: 2ᵈ Crofs'd bef :

Another .

Another crofs'd beh:

1ˢᵗ op: siden: turn: 2ᵈ op: siden :

TABLE of Coupees.

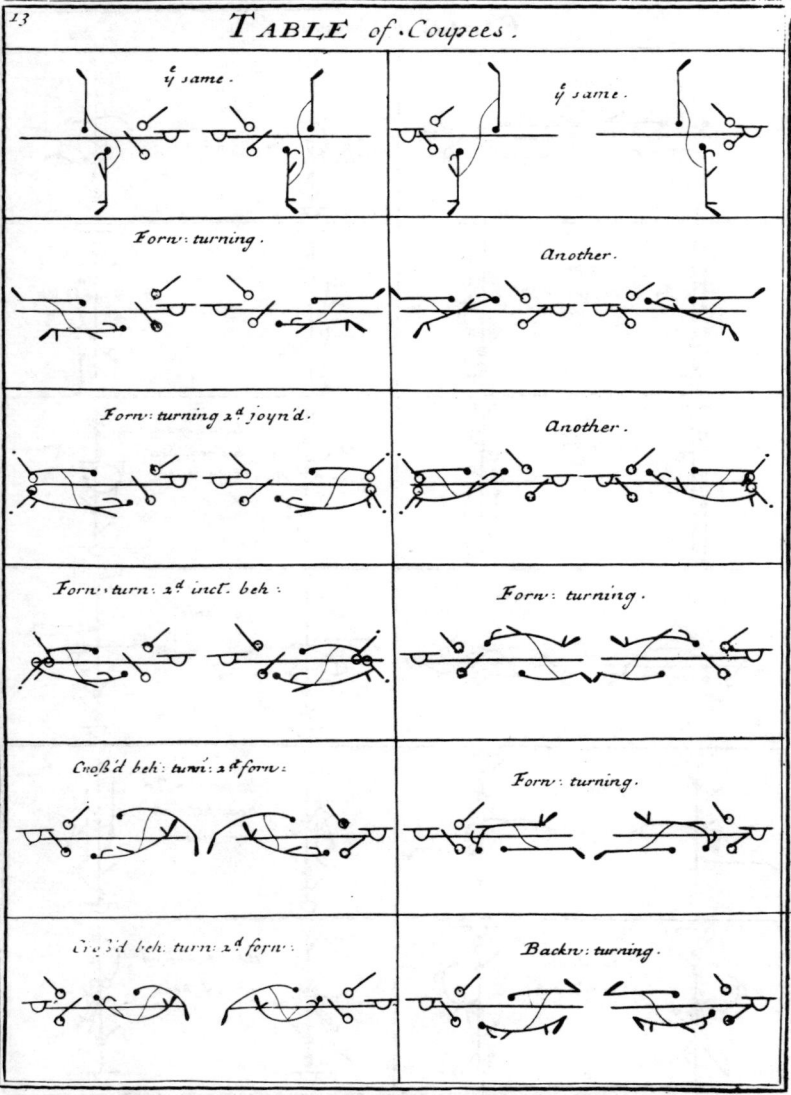

ỹ same.

ỹ same.

Forw: turning.

Another.

Forw: turning 2ᵈ joyn'd.

Another.

Forw: turn: 2ᵈ incl: beh:

Forw: turning.

Cross'd beh: turn: 2ᵈ forw:

Forw: turning.

Cross'd beh: turn: 2ᵈ forw:

Backw: turning.

TABLE of Coupees.

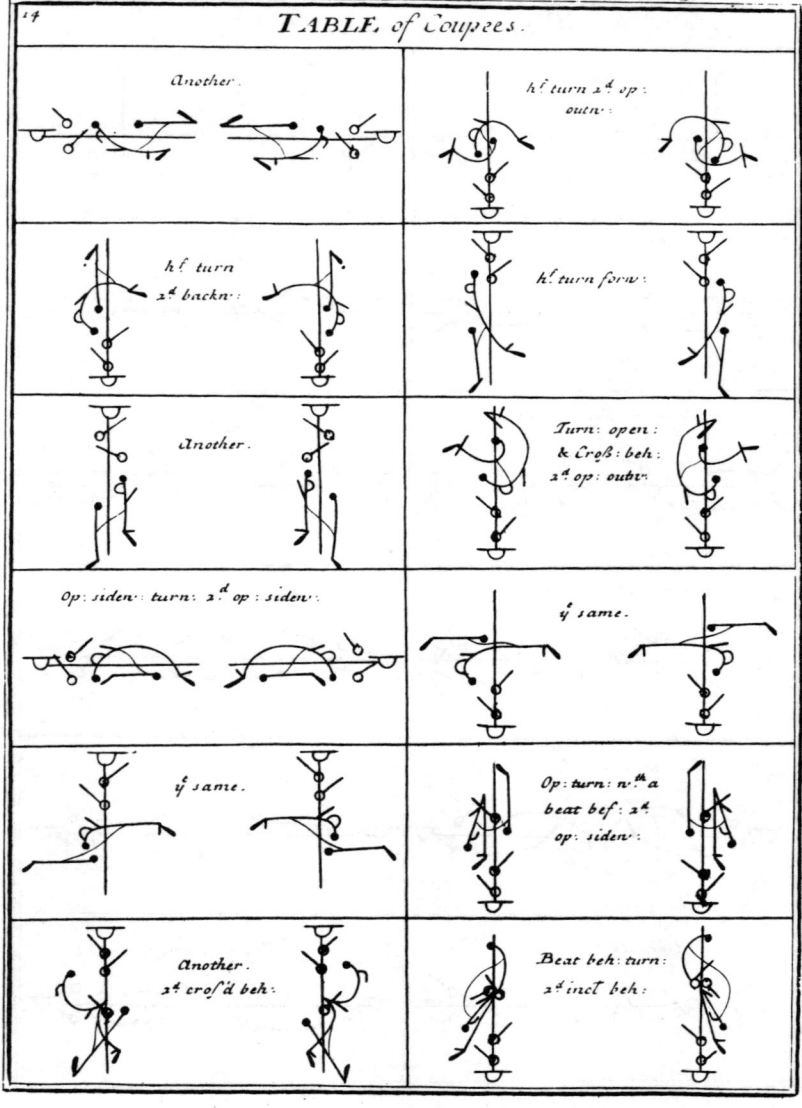

Another.

h.f turn 2.d op: outn:

h.f turn 2.d backn:

h.f turn forw:

Another.

Turn: open: & Croß: beh: 2.d op: outn:

Op: siden: turn: 2.d op: siden:

y.e same.

y.e same.

Op: turn: n.th a beat bef: 2.d op: siden:

Another. 2.d cros'd beh:

Beat beh: turn: 2.d incl: beh:

TABLE of Coupees.

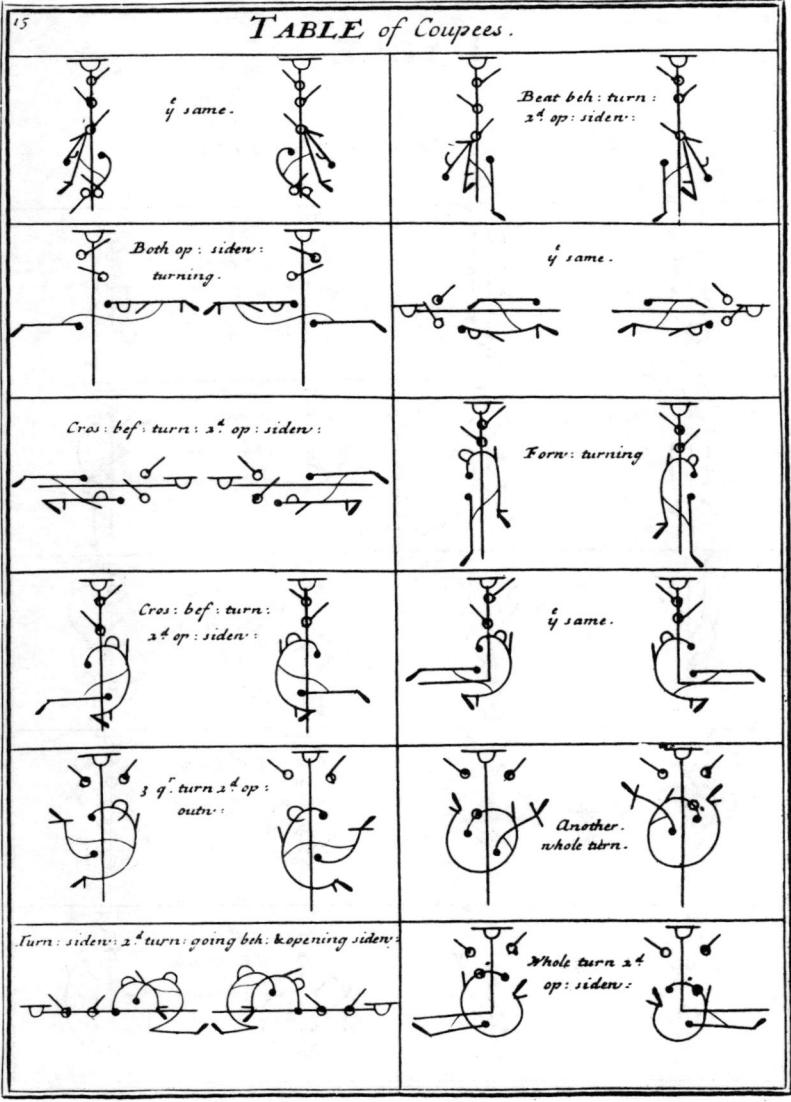

ye same.

Beat beh: turn: 2d op: siden:

Both op: siden: turning.

ye same.

Cros: bef: turn: 2d op: siden:

Forn: turning

Cros: bef: turn: 2d op: siden:

ye same.

3 qr. turn 2d op: outn:

Another. whole turn.

Turn: siden: 2d turn: going beh: & opening siden:

Whole turn 2d op: siden:

TABLE

of

Bouree *steps or* Fleurets

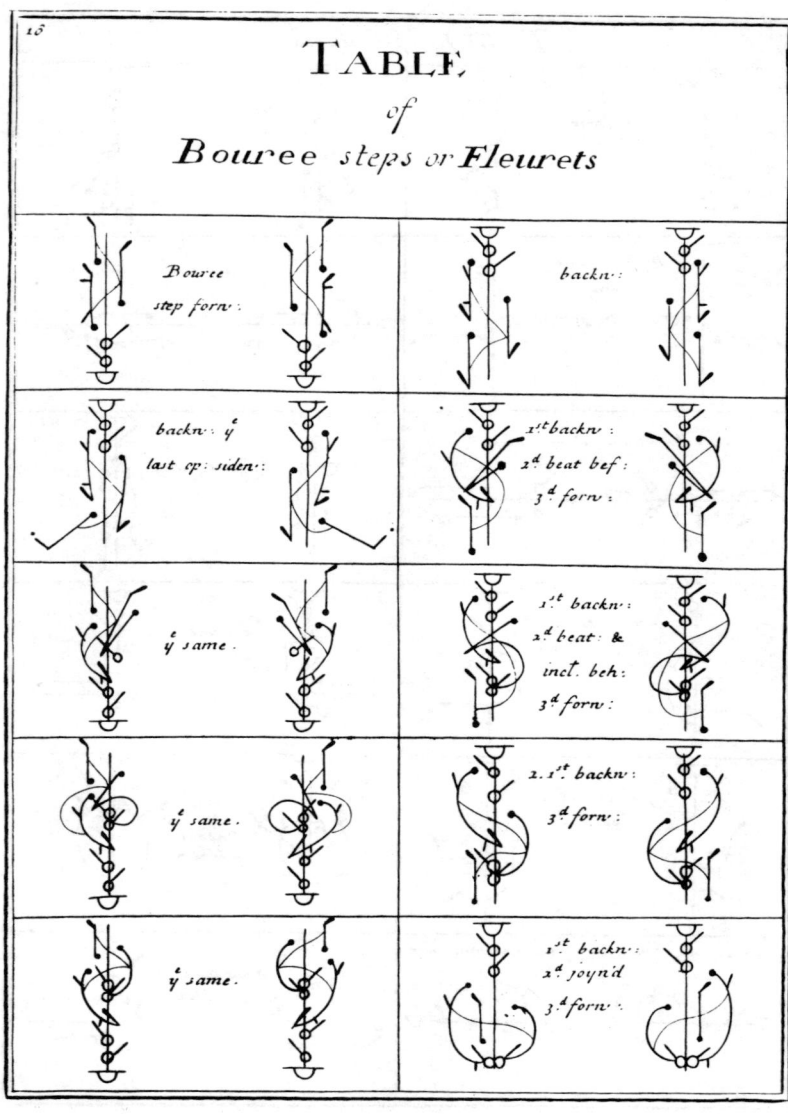

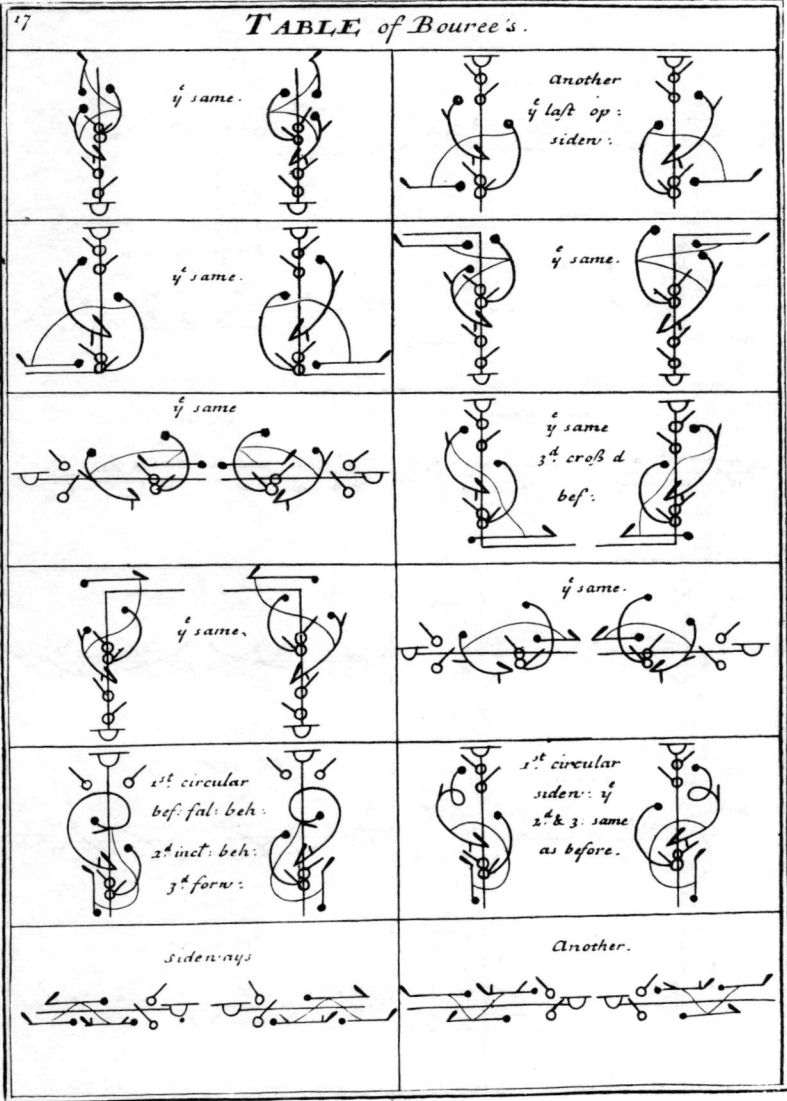

TABLE of Bouree's.

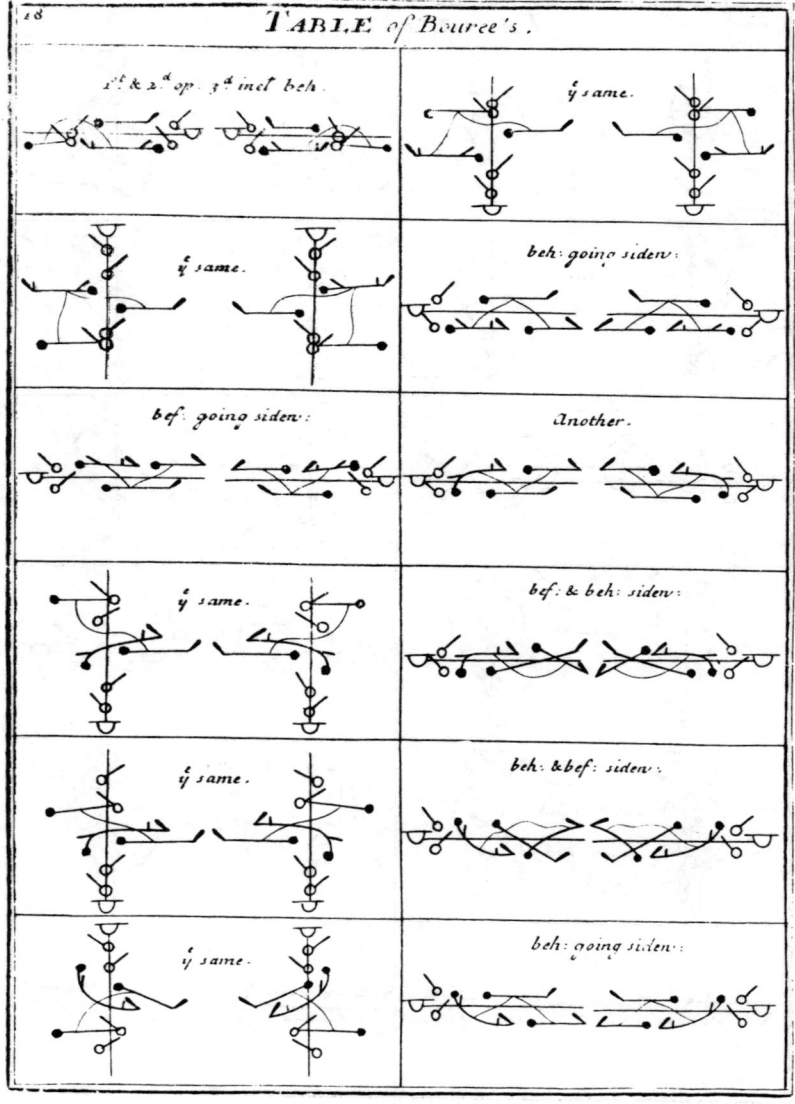

1st & 2d op. 3d incl beh.

ye same.

ye same.

beh: going siden:

bef: going siden:

Another.

ye same.

bef: & beh: siden:

ye same.

beh: & bef: siden:

ye same.

beh: going siden:

TABLE of Bourée's.

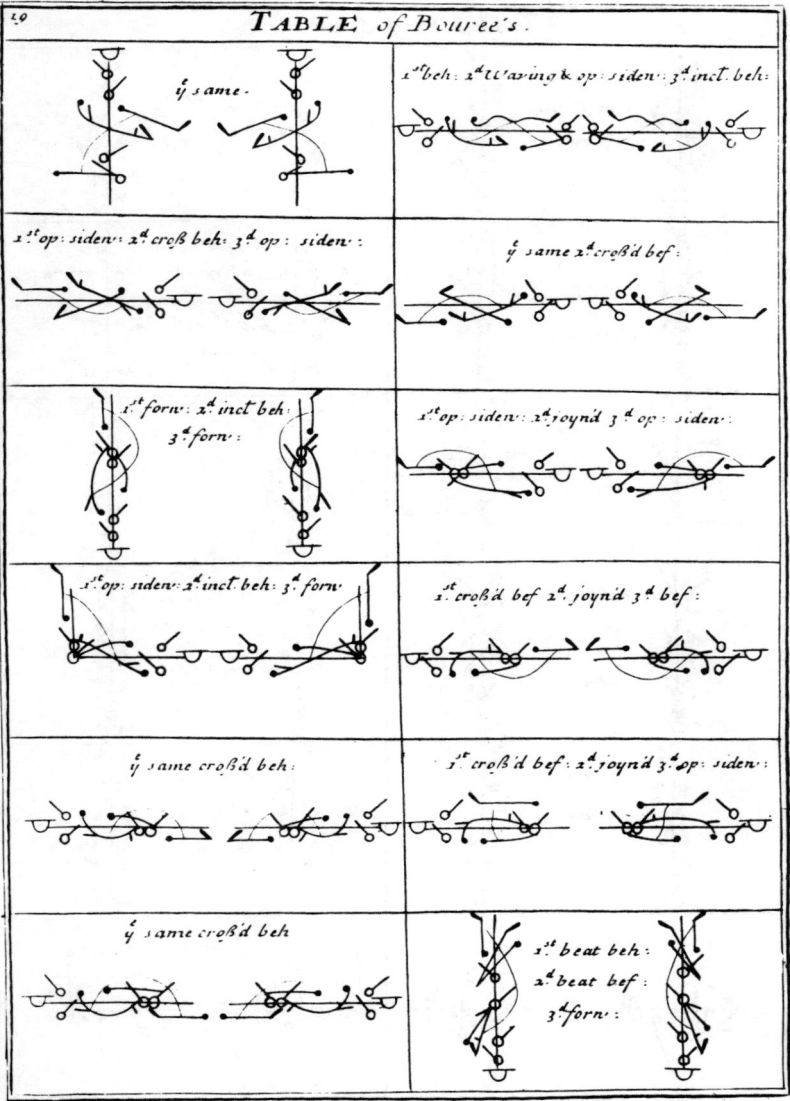

y^e same.

1st beh: 2^d Waving & op: siden: 3^d inct: beh:

1st op: siden: 2^d croß beh: 3^d op: siden:

y^e same 2^d croß'd bef:

1st forn: 2^d inct beh: 3^d forn:

1st op: siden: 2^d joyn'd 3^d op: siden:

1st op: siden: 2^d inct beh: 3^d forn:

1st croß'd bef 2^d joyn'd 3^d bef:

y^e same croß'd beh:

1st croß'd bef: 2^d joyn'd 3^d op: siden:

y^e same croß'd beh

1st beat beh:
2^d beat bef:
3^d forn:

TABLE of Bourée's.

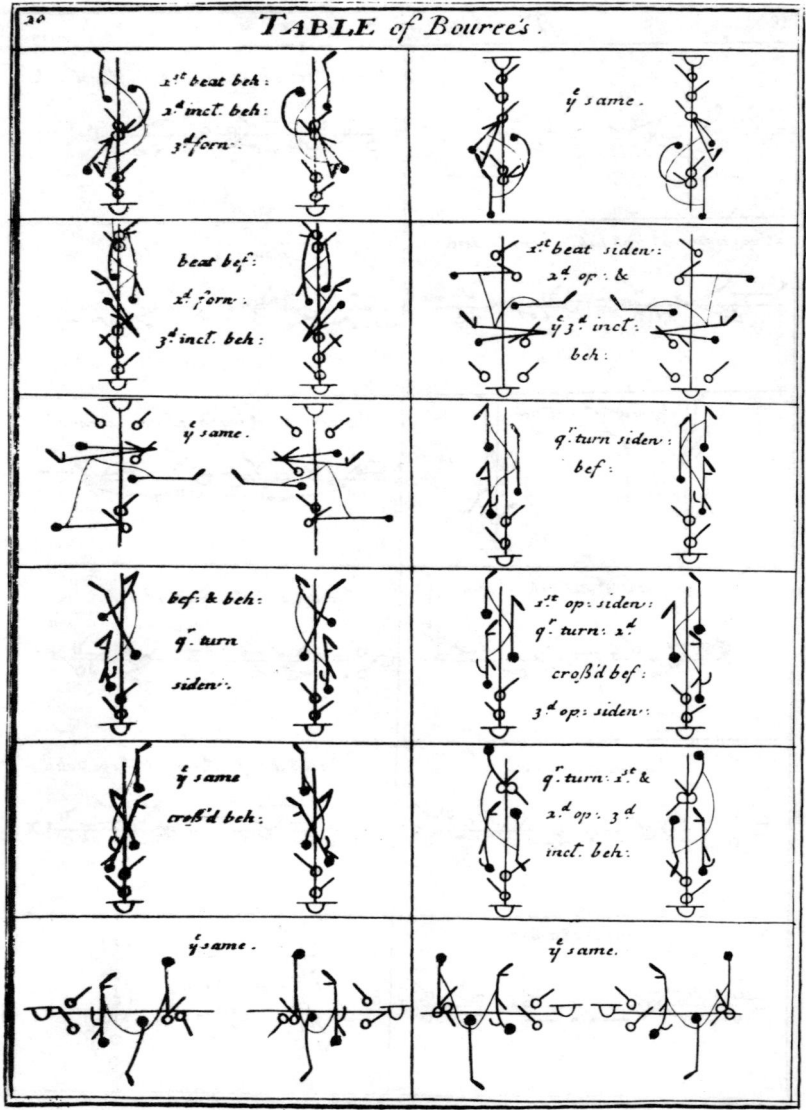

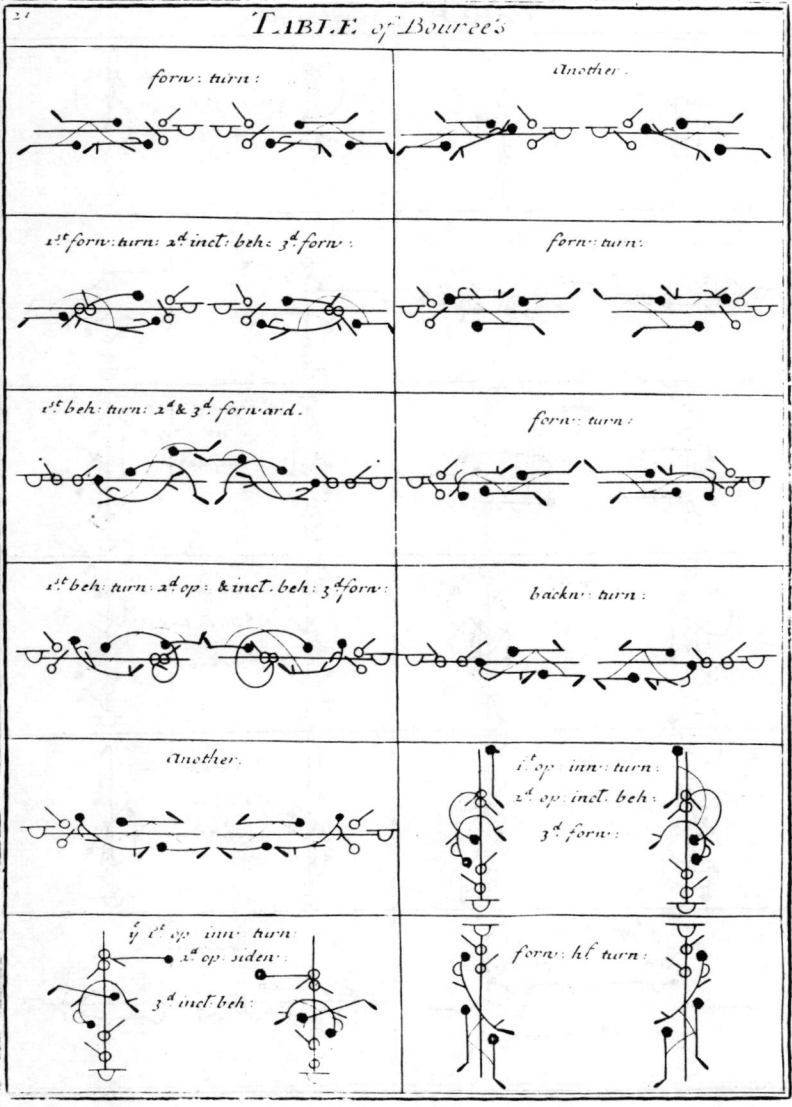

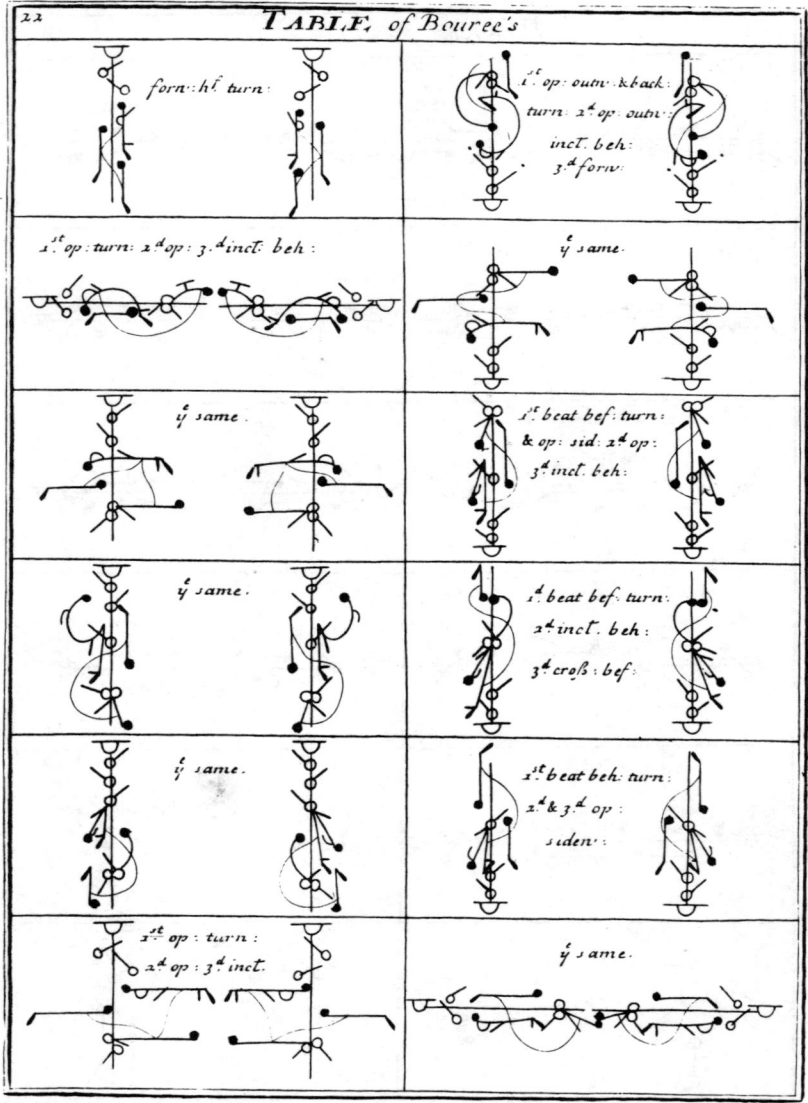

TABLE, of Bourees.

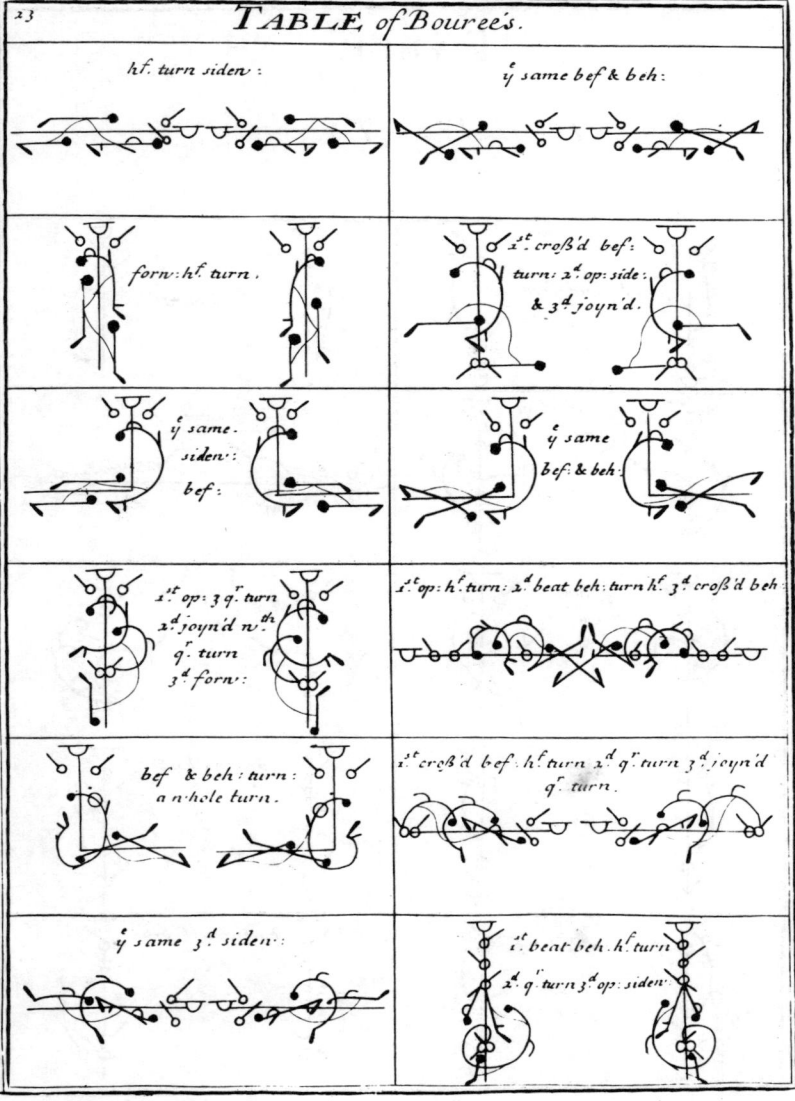

hf. turn siden :

ẏ same bef & beh :

forn : hf. turn .

1ˢᵗ croß'd bef :
turn : 2ᵈ op : side :
& 3ᵈ joyn'd .

ẏ same .
siden ::
bef :

ẏ same
bef : & beh :

1ˢᵗ op : 3 qʳ. turn
2ᵈ joyn'd nᵗʰ
qʳ. turn
3ᵈ forn :

1ˢᵗ op : hf. turn : 2ᵈ beat beh : turn hf. 3ᵗ croß'd beh :

bef : & beh : turn :
a nᵒ hole turn .

1ˢᵗ croß'd bef : hf. turn 2ᵈ qʳ. turn 3ᵈ joyn'd
qʳ. turn .

ẏ same 3ᵈ siden ::

1ˢᵗ beat beh. hf. turn
2ᵈ qʳ. turn 3ᵈ op : siden :

TABLE

of

Bounds or Tacs

a Bound forw:	backwards
op: backw: 2ᵈ op: in ÿ same time.	ÿ same.
ÿ same circul: bef	ÿ same circut: sidew
forw: joyn'd on both feet	ÿ same back:
forw: inclos'd bef	backw: incl: beh:

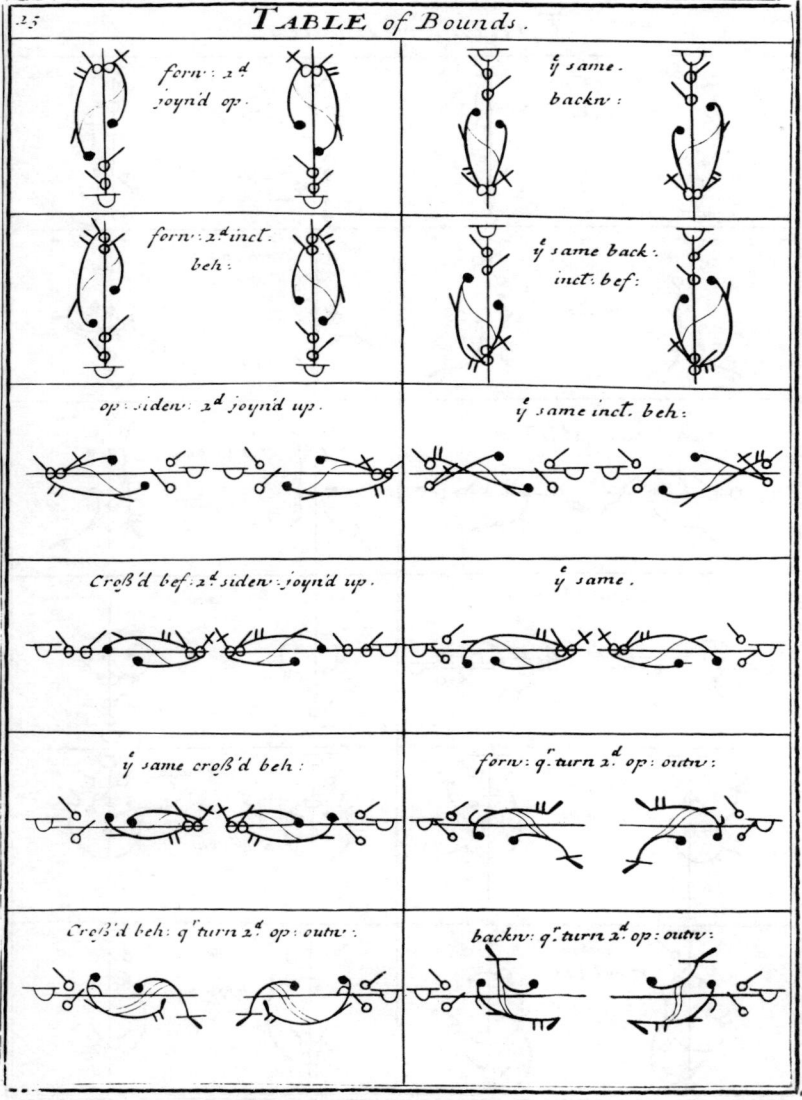

forn:: 2.^d joyn'd op.

ỷ same. backn::

forn:: 2.^d incl. beh::

ỷ same back:. incl: bef::

op:: siden:: 2.^d joyn'd up.

ỷ same incl. beh::

Cross'd bef: 2.^d siden:: joyn'd up.

ỷ same.

ỷ same cross'd beh::

forn:: q.^r turn 2.^d op:: outn::

Cross'd beh:: q.^r turn 2.^d op:: outn::

backn:: q.^r turn 2.^d op:: outn::

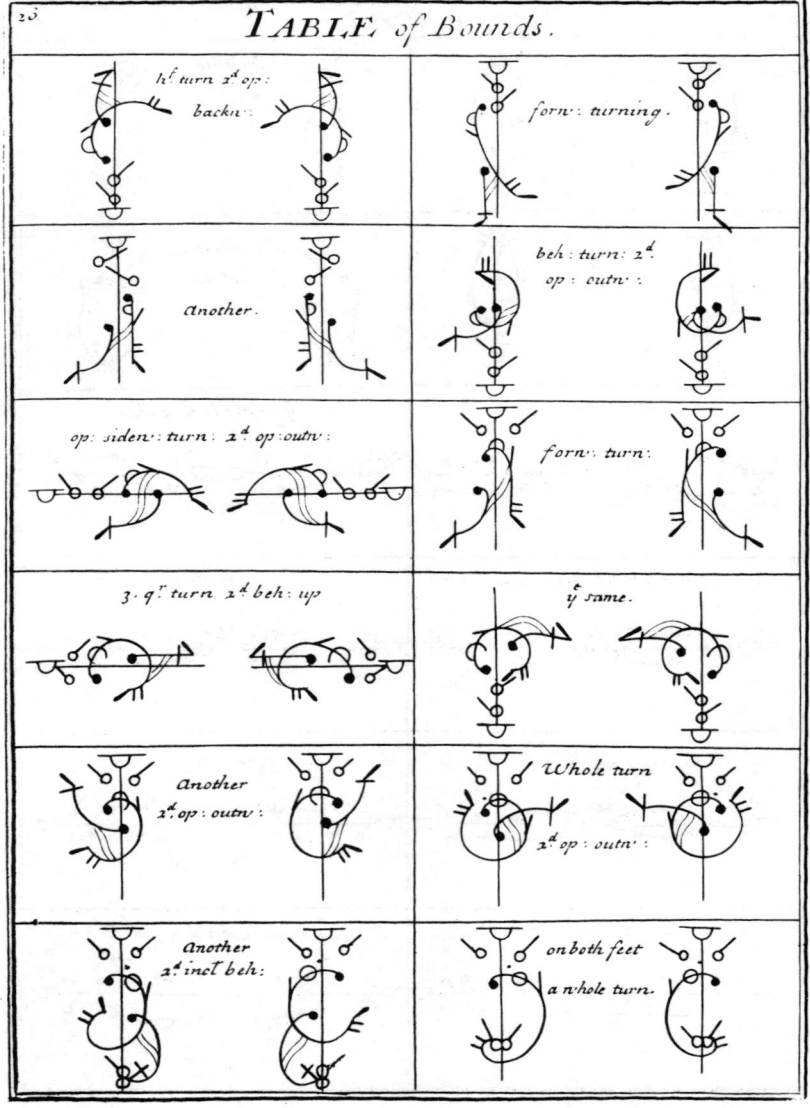

TABLE of Bounds.

27

A TABLE
of
Compos'd Hops or Contretemps.

Contretemps forwards.

backwards.

beat beh & then forn:

beat on ý anckle & forn:

beat on ý ankle 2ᵈ beat beh:

ý same:

backn. 2ᵈ open.

forn: 1ᵗ beat beh: paß'd bef & op: circular.

forn: croß: 2ᵈ beat beh:

ý same circular inn:

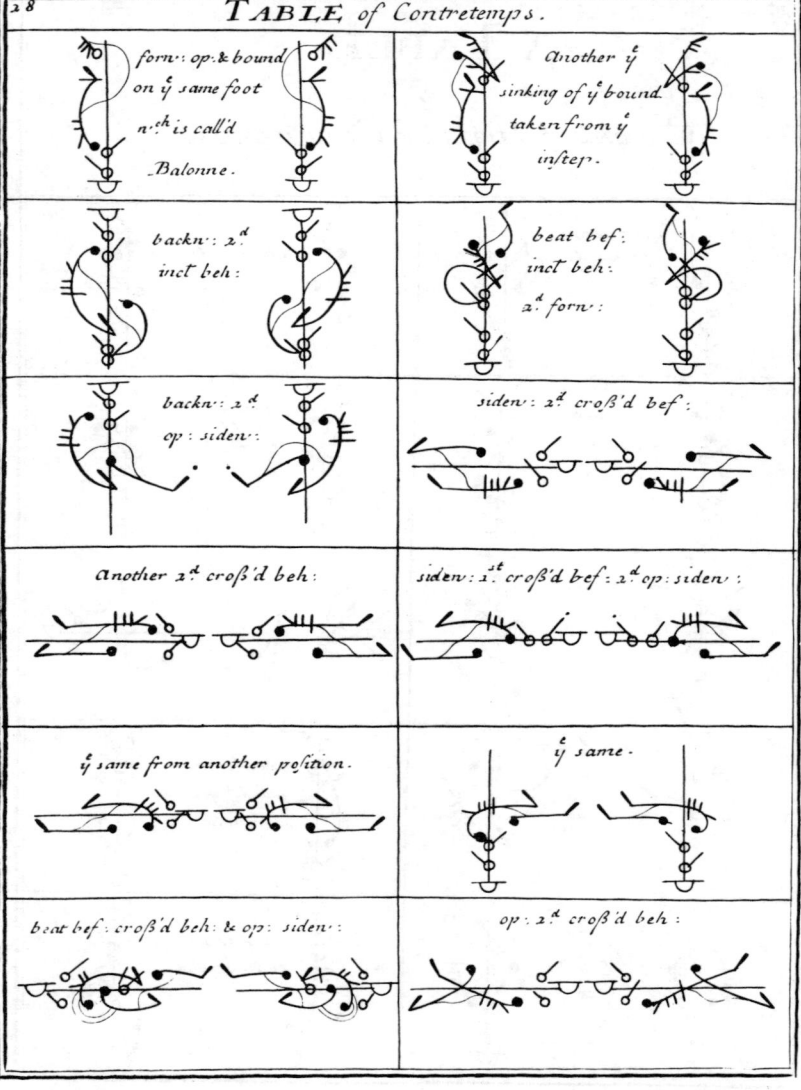

forn: op: & bound on ÿ same foot n:th is call'd Balonne.

Another ÿ sinking of ÿ bound taken from ÿ instep.

backn: 2:d inct beh:

beat bef: inct beh: 2:d forn:

backn: 2:d op: siden:

siden: 2:d croß'd bef:

Another 2:d croß'd beh:

siden: 1:st croß'd bef: 2:d op: siden:

ÿ same from another position.

ÿ same.

beat bef: croß'd beh: & op: siden:

op: 2:d croß'd beh:

TABLE of Contretemps.

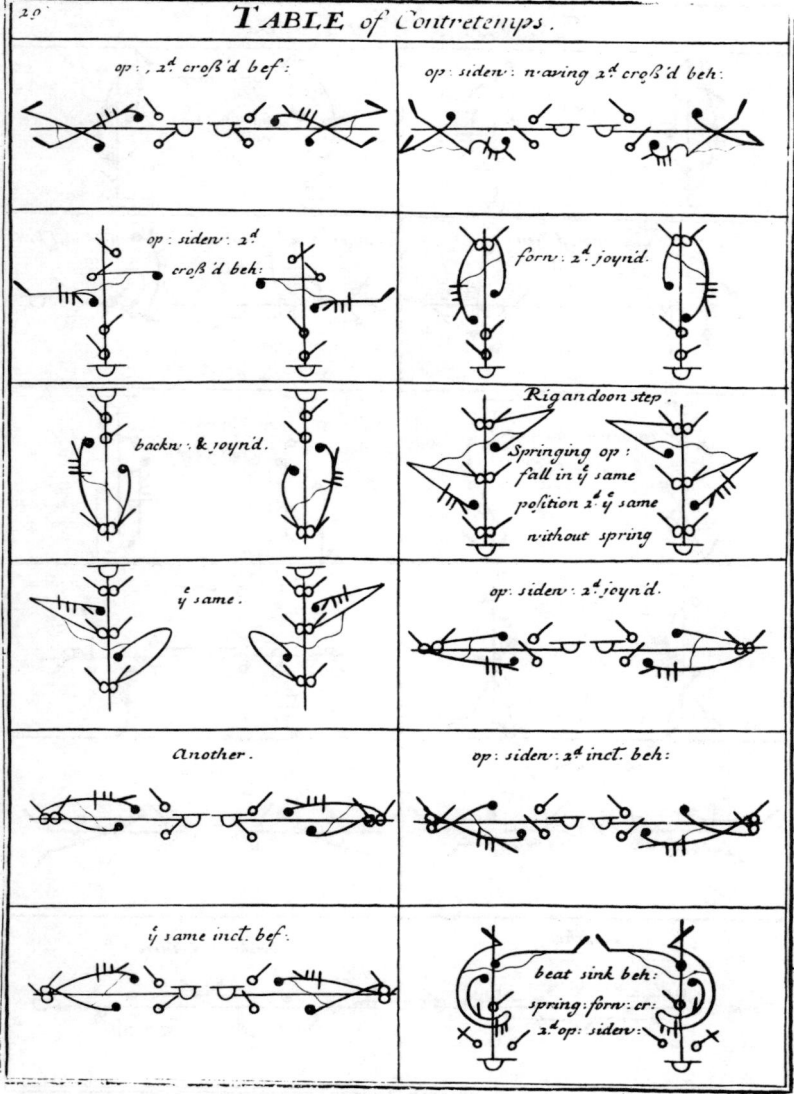

TABLE of Contretemps.

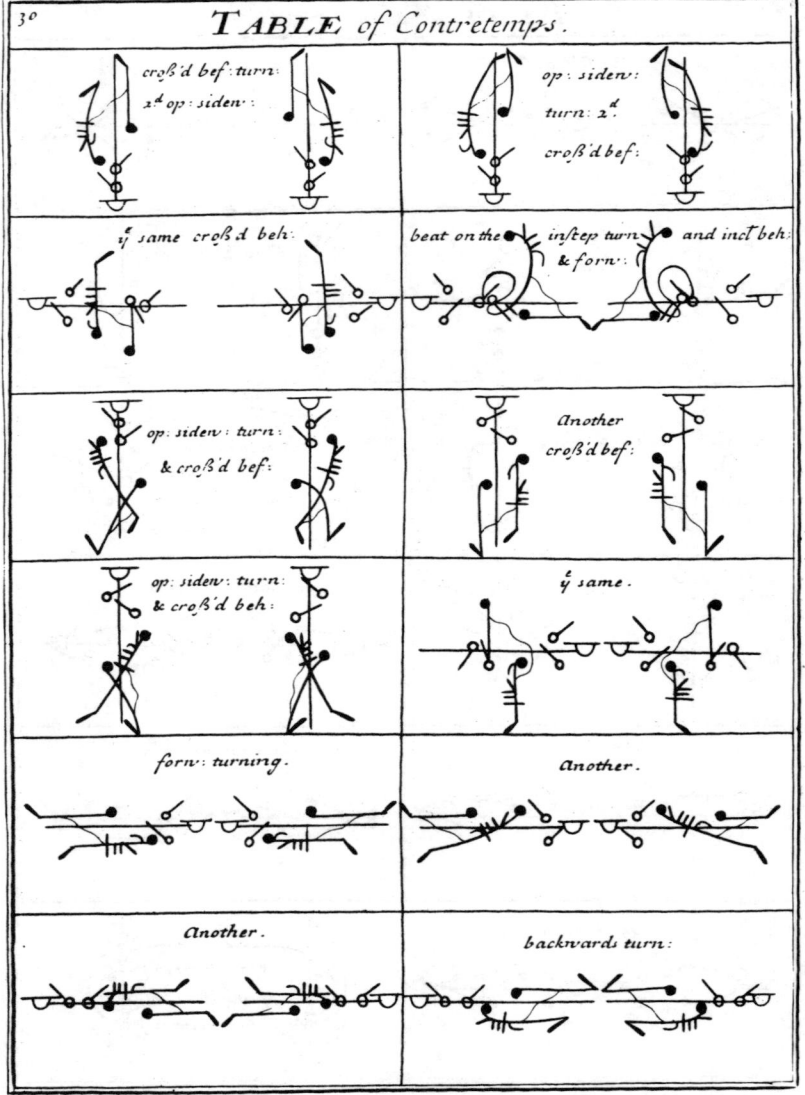

TABLE of Contretemps.

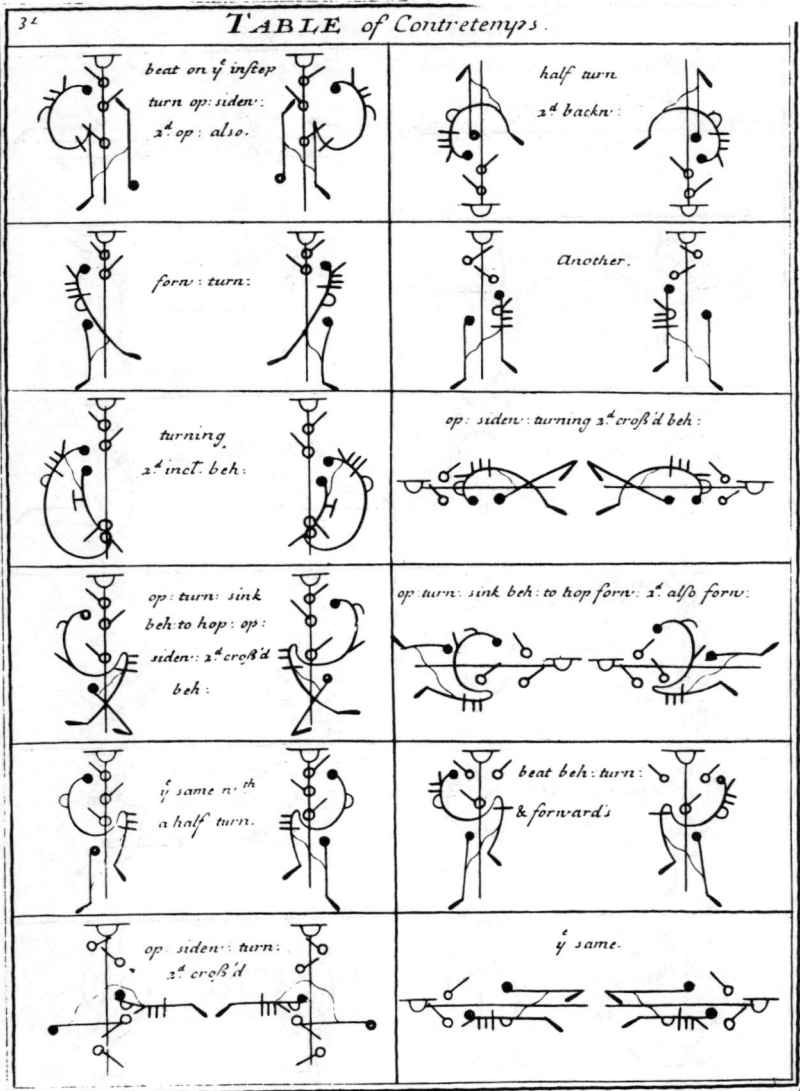

beat on y.e instep
turn op: siden:
2.d op: also.

half turn
2.d backn:

forv: turn:

Another.

turning.
2.d incl: beh:

op: siden: turning 3.d cross'd beh:

op: turn: sink
beh: to hop: op:
siden: 2.d cross'd
beh:

op: turn: sink beh: to hop forv: 2.d also forv:

y.e same n.th
a half turn.

beat beh: turn:
& forvard's

op: siden: turn:
2.d cross'd

y.e same.

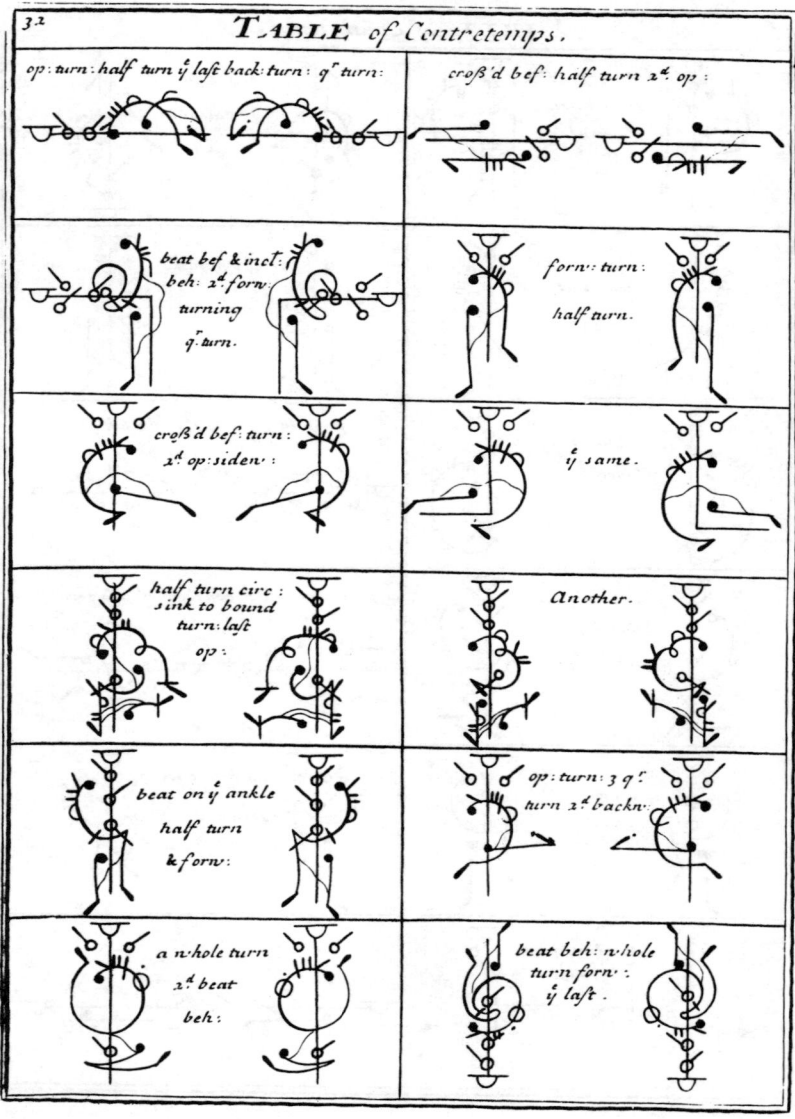

op: turn: half turn ẙ last back: turn: q̃ turn:

croß'd bef: half turn 2ᵈ. op:

beat bef & incl: beh: 2ᵈ forn turning q̃ turn.

forn: turn: half turn.

croß'd bef: turn: 2ᵈ op: siden:

ẙ same.

half turn circ: sink to bound turn: last op:

Another.

beat on ẙ ankle half turn & forn:

op: turn: 3 q̃: turn 2ᵈ backn:

a whole turn 2ᵈ beat beh:

beat beh: whole turn forn: ẙ last.

TABLE

of

Chaßés or Drives.

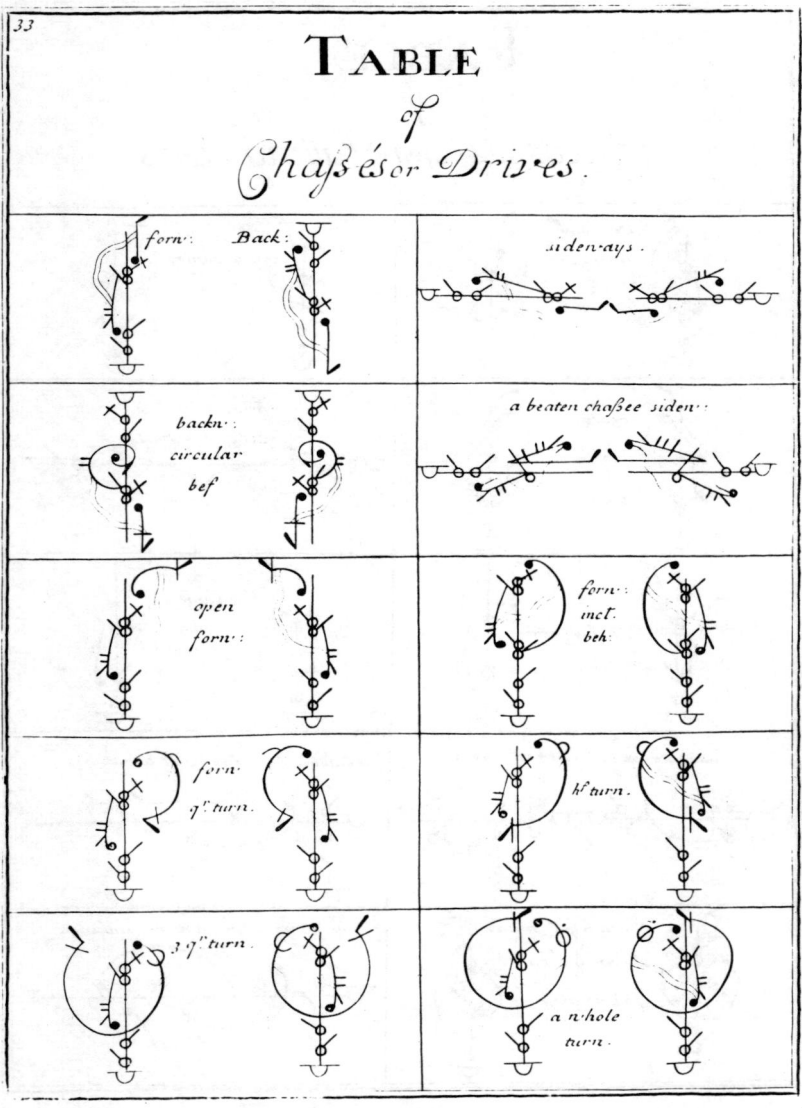

TABLE

of

Chaſsees and Falling steps.

Drive w.th out springing

ye same.

beaten Chaſsee beh:

siden: turn:

Chaſsee forn: w.th falling step.

ye same.

a falling step op both feet & rife on ye 2.d.

Another. 1.st drives ye 2.d & batone.

1.st drives ye 2.d spring: 2.d drive ye 3.d by a falling step.

ye same siden: without sinking.

a TABLE

of

Sissonnes or Cross leaps

Sissonnes forn:

backn:

forn:
2.d op:beh:

forn:

forn: turn: q.r turn.

Another

backn: turn: q.r turn:

hf. turn.

beat return | bef: beh:

ÿ half | same turn.

beat half return | beh: turn beh:

Another half | turn turn:

TABLE
of
Piroüettes.

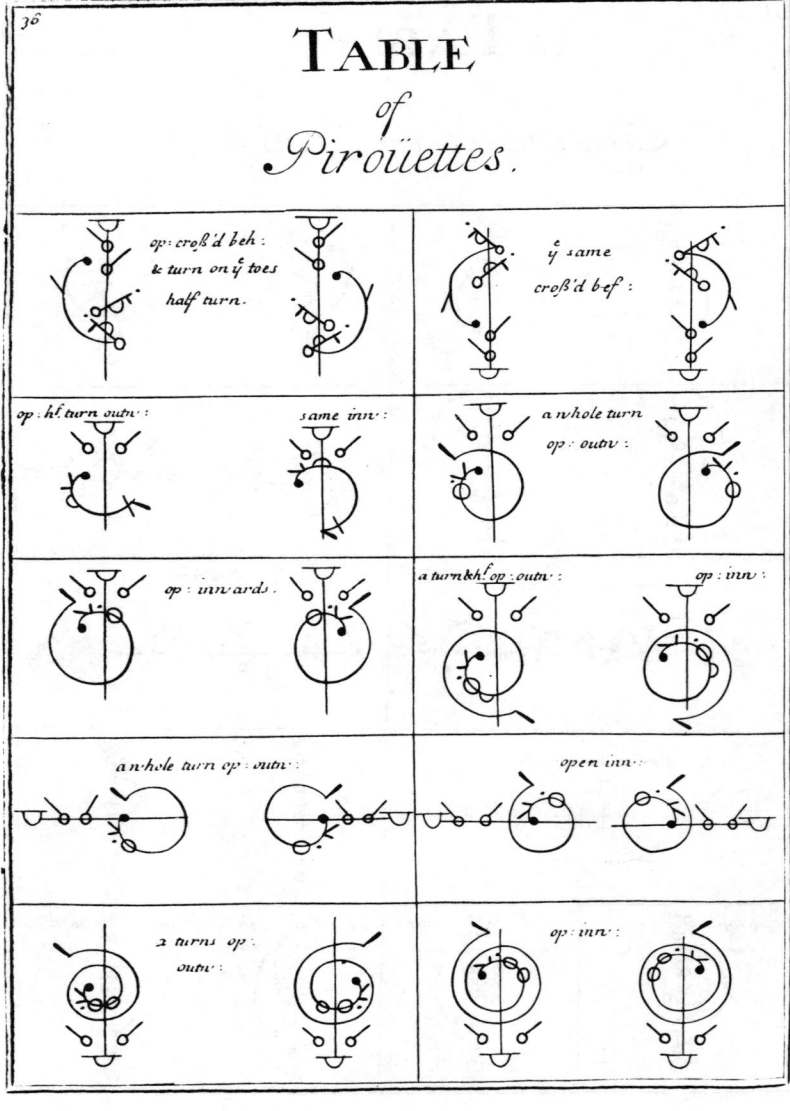

op: croß'd beh:
& turn on ý toes
half turn.

ý same
croß'd bef:

op: hf turn outw:

same inn:

a whole turn
op: outw:

op: innwards.

a turn &hf op: outw:

op: inn:

a whole turn op: outw:

open inn:

2 turns op:
outw:

op: inn:

beat bef: beh: & bef: half a turn outw:

ỹ same innwards

Another outw:

op: a half turn inn: circut: & beating on ỹ instep.

beat bef: beh: & bef: a whole turn outw:

ỹ same inn:

Another outw:

beat bef & beh: one turn r'ov: op: one leg outw:

beat bef: &beh: 2ᵈ each & end incl beh: an hole turn outw:

ỹ same inn:

beat beh: & bef twice each one turn outw:

op: circut: inn: beat bef: beh: & bef: one turn outw:

a TABLE
of
Capers & half Capers.

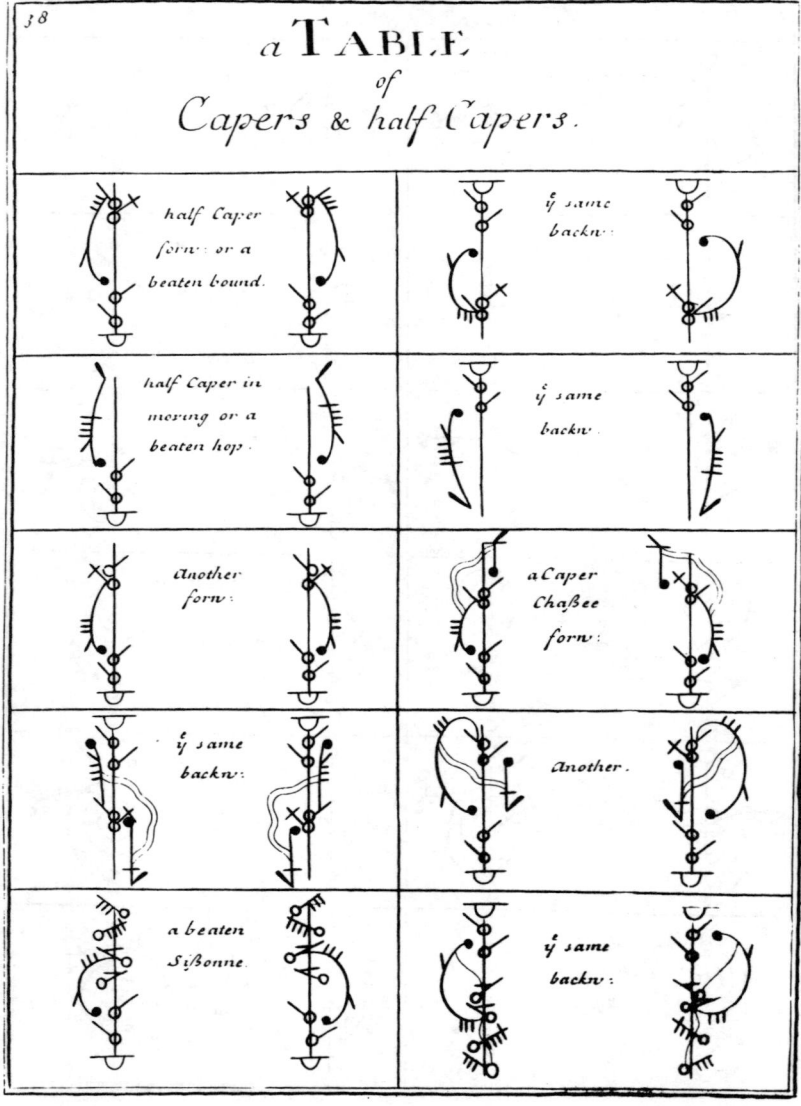

half Caper forn: or a beaten bound.	ỹ same backn:
half Caper in moving or a beaten hop.	ỹ same backn.
Another forn:	a Caper Chaßee forn:
ỹ same backn:	Another.
a beaten Sißonne.	ỹ same backn:

TABLE, of Capers.

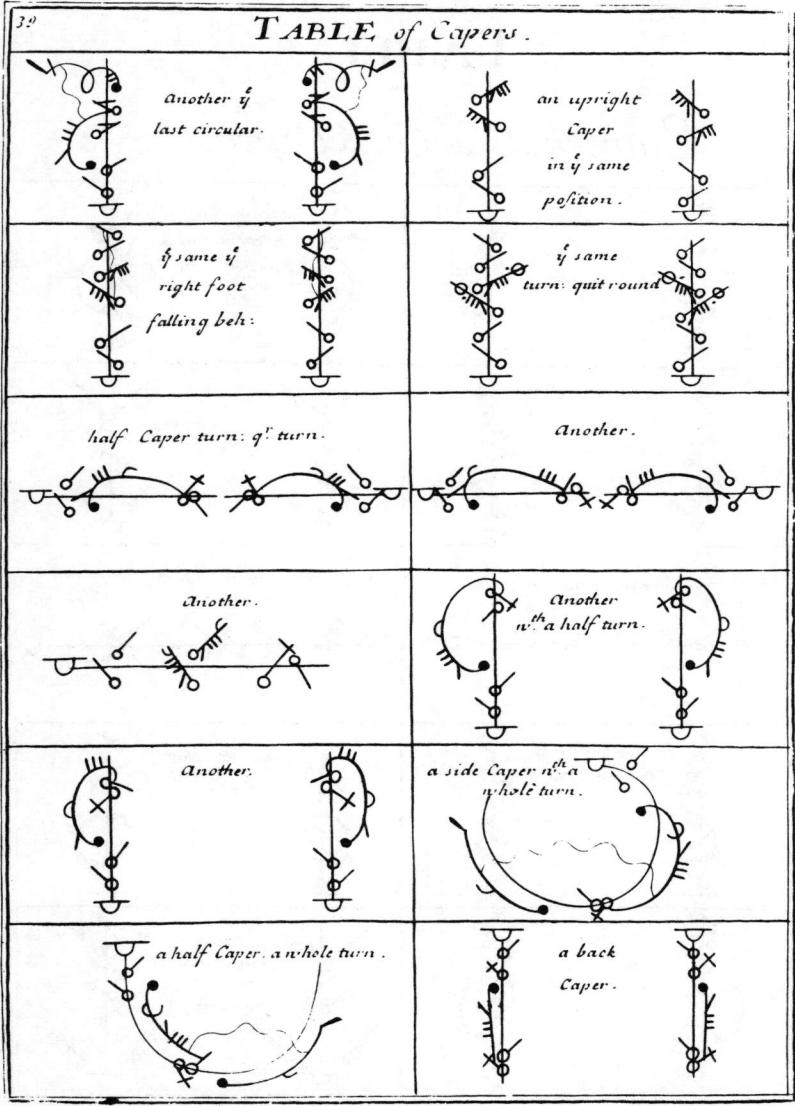

Another ye last circular.

an upright Caper in ye same position.

ye same ye right foot falling beh:

ye same turn: quit round

half Caper turn: qr. turn.

Another.

Another.

Another nth a half turn.

Another.

a side Caper nth a whole turn.

a half Caper. a whole turn.

a back Caper.

a TABLE
of
Entrechats *or* Croß Capers

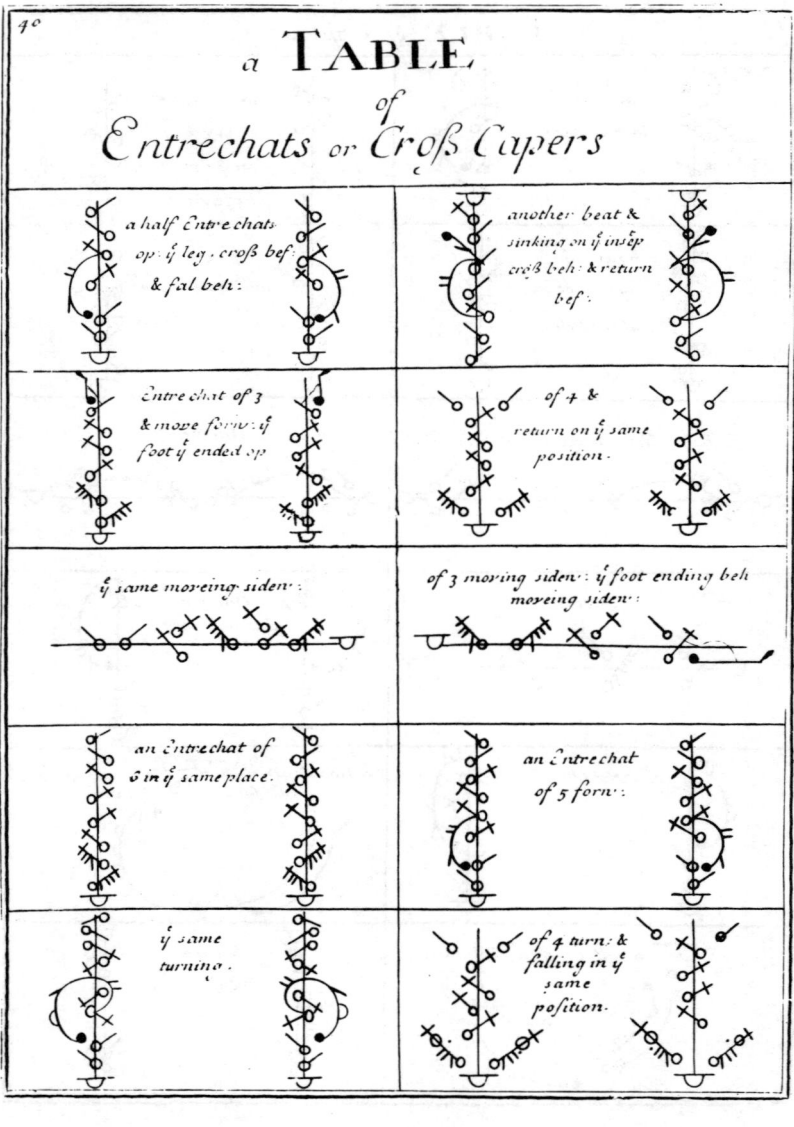

a half Entrechats op: ÿ leg. croß bef: & fal beh:

another beat & sinking on ÿ insép croß beh: & return bef:

Entrechat of 3 & move forw: ÿ foot ÿ ended op

of 4 & return on ÿ same position.

ÿ same moveing siden: :

of 3 moving siden: : ÿ foot ending beh moveing siden: :

an Entrechat of 6 in ÿ same place.

an Entrechat of 5 forn: :

ÿ same turning.

of 4 turn: & falling in ÿ same position.

4.2

TABLE

of

Waving Steps

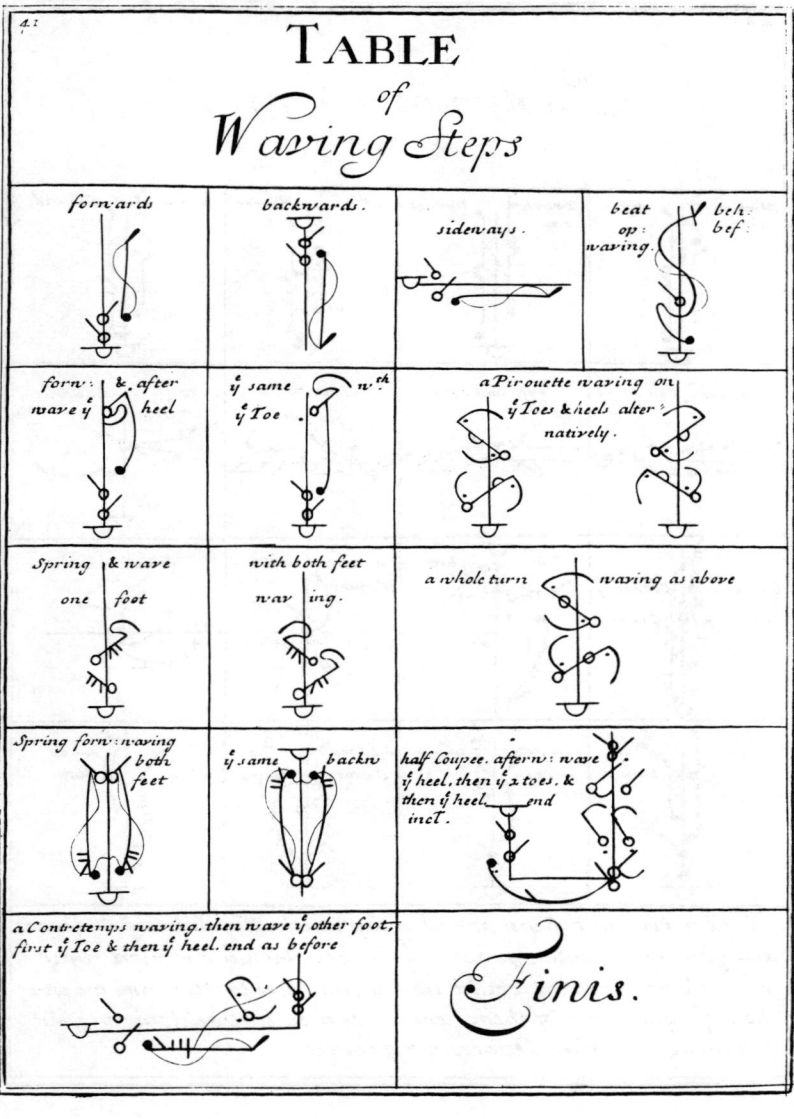

forwards	backwards.	sideways.	beat op: waving. / beh: bef:
forn: & after wave ỿ heel	ỿ same wth ỿ Toe .	a Pirouette waving on ỿ Toes & heels alter: natively.	
Spring & wave one foot	with both feet wav ing.	a whole turn waving as above	
Spring forn: waving both feet	ỿ same backn	half Coupee. aftern: wave ỿ heel. then ỿ 2 toes. & then ỿ heel end incl.	
a Contretemps waving. then wave ỿ other foot, first ỿ Toe & then ỿ heel. end as before		*Finis.*	

a
Suplement of Steps

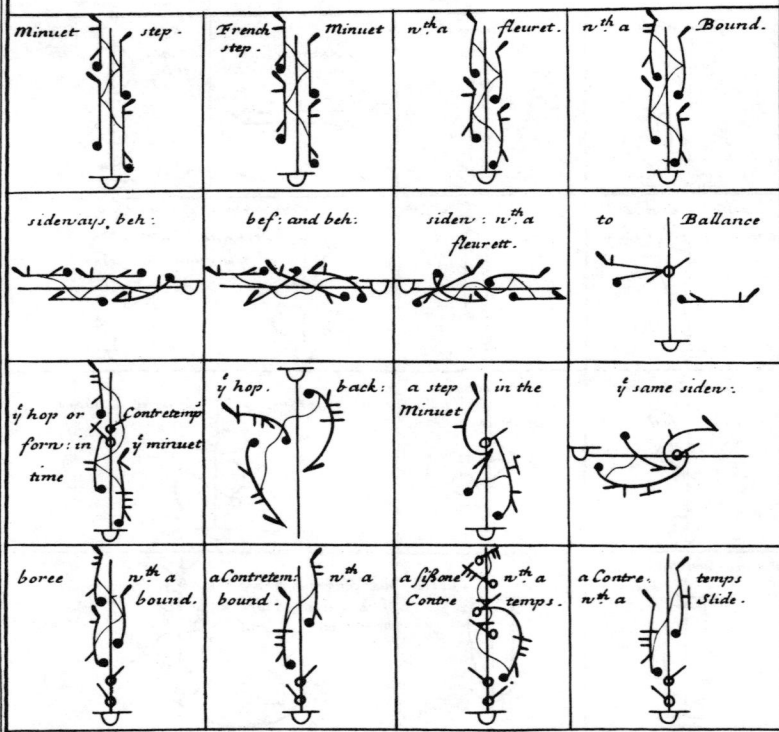

Minuet step.	French step. Minuet	w.th a fleuret.	w.th a Bound.
sideways, beh:	bef: and beh:	siden : w.th a fleurett.	to Ballance
y.e hop or forn: in y.e minuet time	Contretemp	y.e hop. back:	a step in the Minuet	y.e same siden:.
boree w.th a bound.	a Contretem: w.th a bound.	a sißone Contre w.th a temps.	a Contre. w.th a temps Slide.

These four last steps are all of them in the Rigandon. of M.r Isaac's, and give a particular grace to y.e dance. which y.e common way of performing them would not do; and it is to M.r Isaac we owe the so frequent use of them here since they are seldom, or ever found. in any other Dances whatsoever.

Of Time, Measure, or Cadence.

THERE are three forts of *Time* in *Dancing, viz. Common Time, Triple Time,* and *Quadruple Time.*

Common Time, is used in *Gavots, Galliards, Bouree's, Rigandons, Jiggs,* and *Canaries.*

Triple Time, is made use of in *Courants, Sarabands, Chaconnes, Paffacailes, Minuets,* and *Paffe-Pieds.*

And *Quadruple Time,* is made use of in flow *Tunes,* as appears by the fecond *Tune* in the following Plate, and the *Tunes* call'd *Loures.*

To *Tunes* of *Common* or *Triple Time,* a *Step* is put for each *Barr* or *Meafure* ; and to *Tunes* of *Quadruple Time,* you muft put two.

It is to be obferv'd neverthelefs, that in *Courant Movements,* two *Steps* are put to each *Barr* or *Meafure* ; the firft of which takes up two parts in three of the *Meafure,* and the fecond takes up the third part ; and in the *Minuet,* one *Step* is put to two *Barrs* or *Meafures.*

The *Barrs* or *Meafures* in *Dances,* muft be mark'd in like manner with thofe in *Mufick, viz.* with little *Barrs* croffing the *Tract,* which are to agree with thofe of the *Tune.*

Example.

You will underftand by the following Examples, how each *Step* agrees with the *Tune* to which they are compos'd.

Common

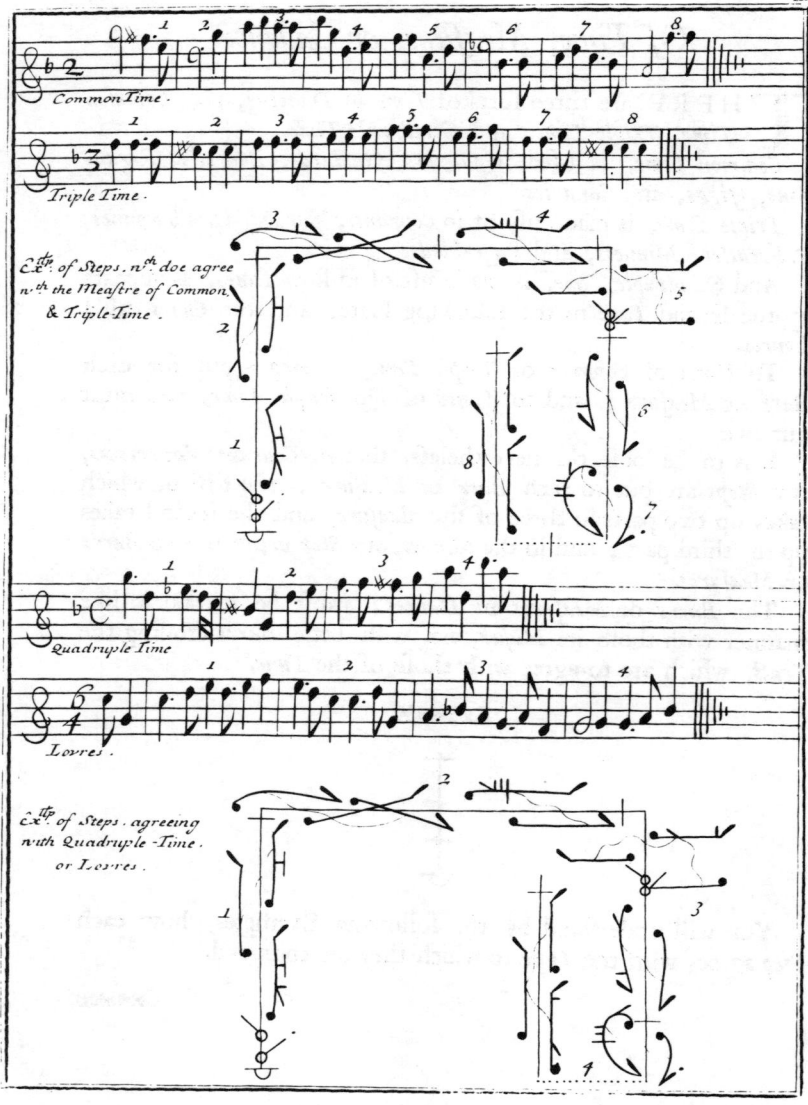

Common Time.

Triple Time.

Ex.tº of Steps. n.tº doe agree
n.tº the Meaſtre of Common
& Triple Time.

Quadruple Time

Lovres.

Ex.tºp of Steps. agreeing
with Quadruple-Time.
or Lovres.

If it happens that you have occasion to put more *Steps* in a *Measure*, than are in the foregoing Examples, the following Rules must be observ'd.

If, for Example, you would in a *Measure* of *Common Time*, or half a *Measure* of *Quadruple Time*, which is the same thing, put a *Fleuret* and a *Bound*; the three *Steps* composing the *Fleuret*, must have a double Tie to join them, and which will shew their Motion to be as swift again, as if there had been but one; the *Bound* also must be join'd to the *Fleuret* with a single Tie only; by which you will know, that these two *Steps* are in Effect but one.

Examples.

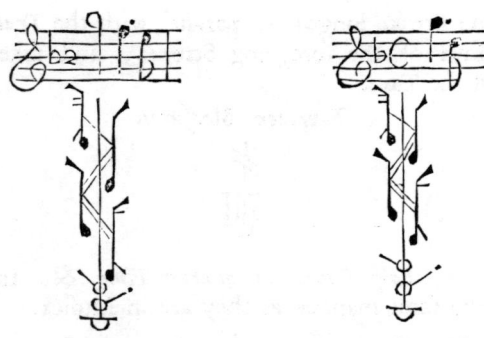

If you would put the same *Step* in a *Measure* of *Triple Time*, the two first *Steps* of the *Fleuret* must only have a double Tie.

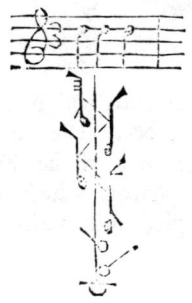

When

When in *Dancing* fome *Meafures* of the *Tune*, are to be let flip, whether in the beginning or middle of the *Dance*, it muft be mark'd in the following manner, *viz.* by a little Stroke croffing obliquely the Tract, and as many of them are to be mark'd, as there are *Barrs* to be let flip ; and in defcribing a half Meafure, half the Stroke only muft be mark'd.

Three Meafures and a half.

The fame Stroke longways, parallel with the *Tract*, is equivalent to four of the foregoing Strokes, and takes up four Meafures of the *Tune*.

Fourteen Meafures.

For a *Time*, *half Time*, or *quarter Time*, &c. they may be mark'd in the fame manner as they are in Mufick.

A quarter Time.
A half Time.
A Time.

In *Tunes*, which begin with odd Notes, as *Gavots*, *Chaconnes*, *Jiggs*, *Loures*, *Bouree's*, &c. the foregoing Marks muft be made Ufe of in the beginning of the *Tract*.

The Letters of the Alphabet, which are plac'd upon the *Steps* in the following Example, and which are alfo plac'd over the

Notes

Notes of the Tune, demonftrate the *Time* or *Cadence* of a Dance.

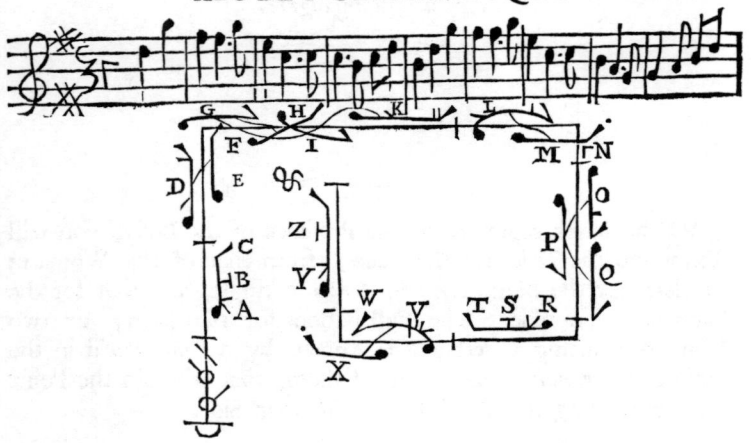

Of the Figure.

THERE are two Sorts of *Figures* in *Dancing*, viz. a *Regular*, and an *Irregular*.

A *regular Figure*, is when two or more *Dancers* move contrarily, the one to the Right, and the other to the Left.

A regular Figure.

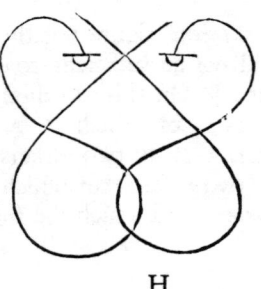

H   An

An *irregular Figure,* is when two *Dancers* move together, both in the fame *Figure,* on the fame fide.

An irregular Figure.

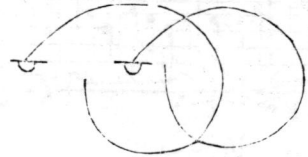

By the Mark reprefenting the Prefence of the Body, you will diftinguifh the *Tract* for the Man, from that of the Woman; in that for the Man, the *half Circle* is fingle, and that for the Woman, is double. The Diftinction for two Men, or two Women Dancing together, is known by a *Point* plac'd in the middle of the *half Circle* of one of them, that wherein the Point is, reprefenting the *Tract* for the Woman Side.

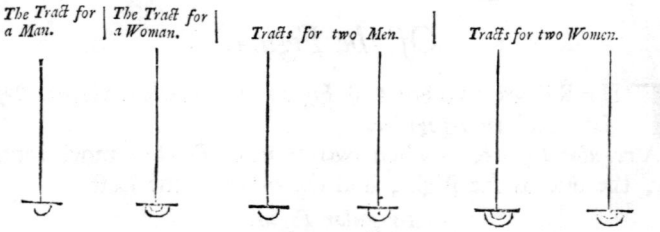

The Tract for a Man.	*The Tract for a Woman.*	*Tracts for two Men.*	*Tracts for two Women.*

If a Number of *Dancers* figure together, the Mark for the placing the Body will not be fufficient to diftinguifh them, (as in a Dance for eight :) On this Occafion therefore, you may make Ufe of Letters, of which A A may reprefent two which figure together. B B two others. C C two more, and D D the other two ; each of which, will alfo be diftin- guifh'd by there *figuring,* and which the following Example will demonftrate.

Some

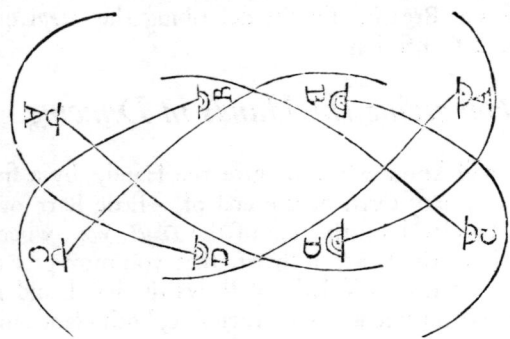

Some Rules to be obferv'd in the Figures of Dances.

I Have already fhewn, that the *Tract* ferves for two Ends, *viz.* firft, on which to defcribe the *Steps* and *Pofitions* ; and fe-condly, for the Direction of the *Figure* of the *Dance.*

I fhall now add, that when in *Dancing,* feveral *Steps* are to be perform'd in the fame place, the *Tract* is then to be refpected only as the Conductor of the *Step,* and not in Relation to the *Figure* ; but where the *Steps* move continually from one place to another, then the *Tract* is to be obferv'd, not only for the Defcription of the *Steps,* but alfo for the *Figure* of the *Dance.* Place your felf then where the beginning of the *Tract* directs, and obferve whether the *Figure* be *ftreight, diametrical, circular,* or *oblique,* whether it be *forwards, backwards,* or *fideways,* if to the right, or to the left ; all which I have already demon-ftrated in the foregoing Pages ; then having learnt the Tune, which muft be prick'd down on the Top of each Page, add the Steps to the Tune, as has been already fhewn, moving in the *Figure* as is defcribed on the Paper. When it happens that the *Tract* or *Tracts* crofs one another, the *Steps* on the one, muft

leave a fufficient Breach, for the defcribing the *Steps* on the o-
ther, to avoid Confufion.

For giving the Hands in Dancing.

OU will know when to give the Hand, by a fmall *Crefcent* or *half Circle* at the end of a little Barr or Stroke,
which is to be plac'd on the fide of the *Tract*, viz. when it is on
the right fide of the *Tract*, it fhews, that you muft give the right
Hand ; and when on the left, it fhews the left Hand is to be
given ; and when there is one on each fide, both Hands muft then
be given.

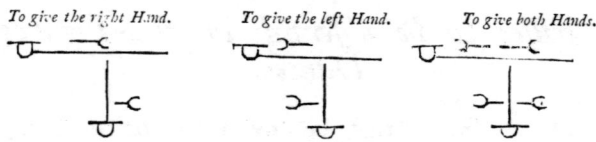

To give the right Hand.   To give the left Hand.   To give both Hands.

When you have thus given one Hand or both, you are not
to quit Hands, 'till you find the fame Marks cut through with
another little Stroke, which fhews, that in that place the Hands
are to let go.

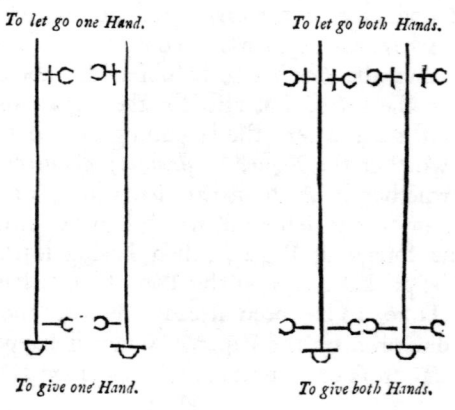

To let go one Hand.   To let go both Hands.

To give one Hand.   To give both Hands.

Of

Of the Movement of the Arms.

ALtho' the Carriage and *Movement* of the *Arms* depend more on the Fancy of the Performer, than on any certain Rules, I fhall neverthelefs lay down fome Examples, which will explain, by demonftrative Characters, the different *Motion* of the *Arms* in *Dancing* ; or at leaft, will inform you what Characters to make Ufe of in defcribing the *Motion* of the *Arms*, to the Movement of each *Step*.

The Arm is reprefented by the Letters A B C, of which A reprefents the Shoulder, B the Elbow, and C the Wrift.

The Arm ftreight.   *The Wrift bent.*   *The Arm bent.*   *The Arm quite before.*

Where to place the Motion of the Arms on the Tract.

IN moving forwards or backwards in the *Dance*, the *Arms* muft be mark'd on each fide the *Tract*, the right *Arm* on the right fide the *Tract*, and the left *Arm* on the left fide ; but when in the *Figure* of the *Dance*, the Movement is fideways, they are to be mark'd both on one fide, always obferving, that the right *Arm* muft be to the right, and the left *Arm* to the left.

Both Arms open. | *The left Arm open, the right bent at Elbow.* | *Both Arms open.* | *The right Arm open, and the left quite clofed in.*

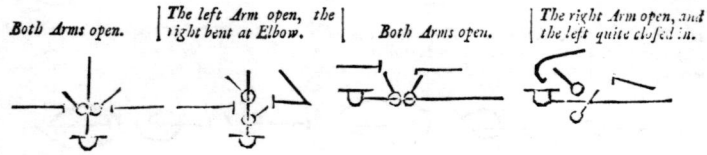

I

I fhall not pretend to make a long Difquifition on the *Moti-*
on of the *Arms*, but fhall only add, that as there are three Movements from the Wafte downwards, fo there are alfo three
Movements in the *Arms*, which have a Correfpondence, and are
agreeing with them below, *viz.* that of the Wrift, has Relation
to the Heel; that of the Elbow, to the Knee, and that of the
Shoulder, or the whole Arm, to the Thigh.

You will know when the Arm moves by an arch'd Line,
mark'd C D, drawn from that which reprefents the end of the
Arm, which fhews the Figure the Wrift makes in moving, as
from C to D.

The *Movements* of the *Arms* are to be perform'd two ways, upwards or downwards; upwards from the *Pofition* of the *Arm*
below, or downwards from the *Pofition* above.

The *Motion* of the *Arm* upwards, is when the *Arm*, which is
open or extended, clofes (in approaching) to the Body afcending,
and the Motion of the *Arm* downwards, is when the *Arm*, which
is clos'd, opens or extends it felf defcending.

Examples of the Movements of the Arms.

The Motion of the Wrift up-wards.	The Motion of the Elbow up-wards.	The Motion of the whole Arm upwards.	The Motion of the Wrift down-wards.	The Motion of the Elbow down-wards.	The Motion of the whole Arm downwards.

The Wrift mo-ving round up-wards.	The Elbow mo-ving round up-wards.	The whole Arm moving round upwards.	The Wrift mo-ving round downwards.	The Elbow mo-ving round downwards.	The whole Arm moving round downwards.

The

The *Wrist* moving round downwards.	The *Elbow* moving round downwards.	The whole *Arm* moving round downwards.	Double Movement of the *Wrist* upwards and downwards.	Double Movement of the *Elbow* upwards and downwards.	Double Movement of the whole *Arm* up. and downw.
		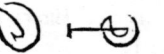			

The *Arms* may either move both together, or one after the other; you will know when the *Arms* are to move together, by a *Line* or *Tie* drawn from the one to the other; and when there is no *Tie*, they are then to move one after the other.

The *Arms* may either move alike with the same Movement, as when both *Arms* either open or extend themselves together, or close, or approach each other at the same time.

Or they may move contrary one to the other, when the one opens, and the other closes.

Both *Arms* moving together with the same Motion.	Both *Arms* moving together with a contrary Movement.	Both *Arms* moving one after the other, first the right, and then the left.
		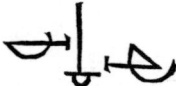

Some Rules to be observ'd in writing of Dances.

YOU must resolve in what part of the *Room* the *Dance* is to begin, and there place the beginning of the *Tract*; then trace out the *Figure*, and mark thereon the *Position*; then describe the *Steps*, as I have shewn in the foregoing Examples; and if you find any Difficulty in writing any of the *Steps*, you must make Use of your *Table* of *Steps*; and in finding the *Step* you have Occasion for, you ought first to consider what *Step* it is, whether *Courant, Coupee, Bouree, Bound, Contretemps,* &c. Suppose, for Example, the *Step* to be a *Bouree,* turn then to the Table of *Bouree's* or *Fleurets,* and having found the *Step* you

want,

want, obferve after what manner it is defcrib'd, and then write
it down in your Dance.

On the Top of each Page, on which your Dance is defcrib'd,
you muft prick down as many Barrs of the Tune, as there are
Barrs or Meafures in the Dance.

Altho' the *Tract* ferves generally for the explaining the *Figure*
of the Dance, yet it often happens that many *Steps* are to be
perform'd in the fame Place, and then (as I have fhewn before)
the *Tract* is to have regard only to the *Steps*. This *Tract* is only a borrow'd *Tract*, and which may be drawn any way, as
fhall be moft convenient. As for Example, from A to B, altho'
the *Tract* is drawn out in length from A to B, the *Dancer* neverthelefs removes not from A, which may alfo be well underftood
by the *Steps*, which are from A to B, which can only be perform'd in the fame place.

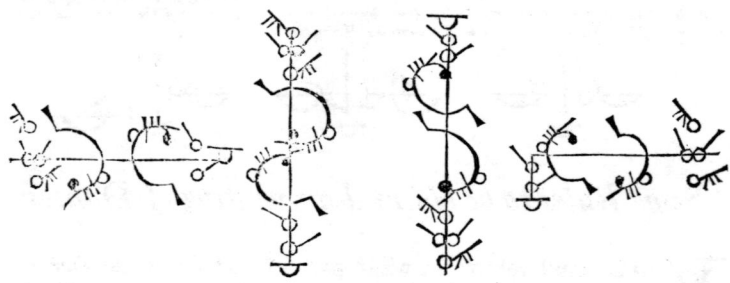

You muft obferve at the end of each Page, the place where the
Dancer finifhes, and to what part of the *Room* the Face directs,
by which means you will readily know where to place the beginning of the *Tract* in the following Page ; and fo continue from
Page to Page, to the end of the *Dance*.

But if in the beginning of a Page, two Dancers fhould happen
to be clofe together, and fome *Steps* to be perform'd in the fame
place ; which *Steps* cannot be conveniently defcribed, neither
on

on one fide, or the other, and that the Clofenefs of the *Dancers*, will not admit of advancing of the *Tracts*, one towards the other; you muft then be oblig'd, inftead of placing the *Tracts* at C D, to retire as far back as will be neceffary to defcribe the *Steps*, fo that the *Steps* may end at C D.

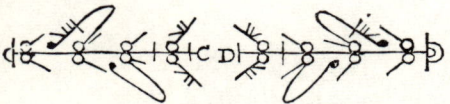

Or elfe the contrary may be done, by placing the beginning of the *Steps* at C D; and inftead of defcribing the *Steps* one towards the other, they muft feparate, as from C to E, and D to F.

You will find thefe are perform'd without the *Dancers* moving out of their Places; and both thefe Examples are equally good, in confidering only which agrees beft with the *Figure* of the *Dance* that follows.

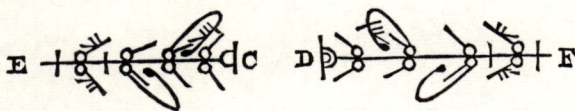

If in the *Dances* in the fecond Volume, you find fome of the *Steps* longer than others, you muft have no Regard to them, as to their Length in the Defcription of them, but judge of their Extenfion by the Diftance of *Pofitions*, (as I have already fhewn in the Termination of the *Steps*, in their *Pofitions*;) fo that you are not to conclude any thing from the Length or Shortnefs of Steps.

F I N I S.

A SMALL

TREATISE

OF

Time and *Cadence*

IN

DANCING,

Reduc'd to an

Eafy and Exact METHOD.

SHEWING

How *Steps*, and their *Movements*, agree
with the *Notes*, and *Divifion* of *Notes*,
in each *Meafure*

By JOHN WEAVER, *Dancing-Mafter.*

LONDON:

Printed by *H. Meere,* at the *Black Fryar,* in *Black Fryars,*
for the Author, and are to be Sold by *Ifaac Vaillant, French* Book-
feller, near *Catherine-Street,* in the *Strand.* 1706.

An Eafy and Exact *Method* for
knowing the *Time* and *Cadence* in *Dancing*.

IN a Treatife entitled *Orchefography*, or, *The Art of Dancing
by Characters*, &c. I have already laid down fome Rules to
be obferv'd in the *Time*, *Cadence*, and *Meafures* of *Dances* :
But having fince met with a more correct and perfect Method of Monfieur *Feuillet'f*, in his late Collection of *Dances*; in
which are feveral Rules and Examples, for a more exact and nice
Obfervation of the *Time*, *Cadence*, and *Meafure* ; and the former
not being fufficient to explain the many Difficulties that may a-
rife, I thought a Publication of this latter would not prove un-
acceptable, it being fo ufeful, and abfolutely neceffary towards a
perfect Knowledge of this *Art*.

It is firft then to be obferv'd, that in the general Rule for
Meafures and *Time* in *Mufick*, two forts of Movements are only
made ufe of, *viz*. *Common Time*, and *Triple Time*, for on thefe depend all the reft ; fome of which are quicker, and fome flower,
yet all to be beat as *Common* and *Triple Time*.

A *Meafure* of *Quadruple Time*, is therefore the fame as two
Meafures of *Common Time*, which I fhall alfo call a *Meafure* of
Two Times, by fuppofing another *Bar* in the middle of the *Meafure*, as is demonftrated by the firft Example following ; and if
in lieu of *Quavers*, you put *Crotchets*, and inftead of *Crotchets*,
you put *Minums*, it will then be two *Meafures* of *Common Time*,
or *Two Times*. as is fhewn in the fecond Example.

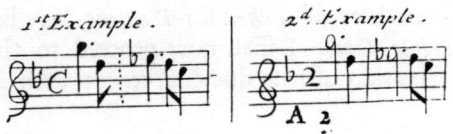

1ᵗ Example.   *2ᵈ Example*.

A 2   A

A *Measure* therefore of *Quadruple Time*, is to be confidered in *Dancing*, as if it were two *Measures* of *Common Time*, or *Two Times*; and this is the Reafon that two *Steps* are put in a *Measure* of a *Tune* of *Quadruple Time*.

The fame Obfervation is alfo to be made on *Loures* and *flow Jiggs*, which contain fix *Crotchets* in a *Measure*; for each *Meafure* of a *Loure* or *flow Jigg*, is the fame with two *Measures* of *Triple Time*; for if you put another Bar in the middle of the *Measure* of a *Loure*, it will be then two *Measures* of *Triple Time*; as for Example.

Loure.

There are ftill other *Movements*, in which each *Measure* may be divided into many others, as thofe frequently ufed by the *Italians*, in their brifk *Movements* of *Quadruple Time*, as is fhewn by the firft Example following.

Thefe fort of *Movements* ought to be confider'd in *Dancing*, as *Measures* of *Triple Time*, like thofe in *Paffe-pieds* or *Minuets*, by obferving each *Measure* in refpect to its Divifion; for if you put Bars between every three *Quavers*, as you may fee by the pointed Lines in the fecond Example following, each *Bar* or *Measure* will produce four *Measures* of a *Paffe-pied*; and if you make *Crotchets* of the *Quavers*, and *Minums* of the *Crotchets*, it will then make four *Measures* of a *Minuet*, as in the third Example.

Having now fhewn how all *Tunes* for *Dancing* may be reduc'd to *Common* and *Triple Time*, I fhall now proceed to the giving Rules for the Obfervation of the due *Cadence* of each *Step*, and how

how the *Steps* in the *Measures* of a *Dance* agree to the Notes of the *Measures* of the *Tune* on which the *Dance* is composed.

The best and only Method of finding the *Cadence* or *Time* of each *Step*, is to know its just Value in the same manner as the Notes of Musick ; after which all the *Steps* in a *Measure*, are to be reduc'd to an equal Time or Length, as the Notes in the Measure of the Tune.

And since I have not found any Method so proper for the understanding the Value of each simple *Step*, than the Tye, which I have already made use of for the making a compofed *Step*, I shall still make use of this Tye ; by explaining which, the just Value of each simple *Step* will be easily demonftrated, by obferving the following Rules.

It is to be obferv'd, as a general Rule, that all fimple *Steps*, which are ty'd together by a fimple Line or Tye, must be all of an equal Length or Value : So that each *Step* fo ty'd, employs a Time of the Meafure of the Tune, as is explain'd in the two Examples following.

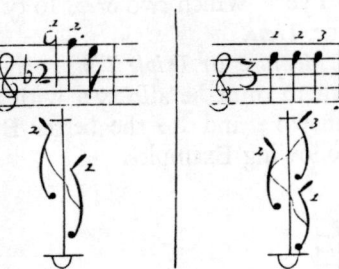

In thefe two Examples, and in all the reft that follow, I have mark'd each *Step* with Figures, for the better explaining their Time and Value, and to fhew more eafily their Correfpondence with the Notes of the Tune : Over which are alfo plac'd the fame Figures.

When it fhall happen that two *Steps* are not quite ty'd, that is to fay, when one end of the Line or Tye does not touch one of

the

the said *Steps*, that *Step* which the Tye does not touch, muſt be as long again in the Performance, as the other *Step*, which the Tye touches, and ought to be conſider'd on this Occaſion, as a *Minum* in Muſick, in a Meaſure of Triple Time.   As for Example.

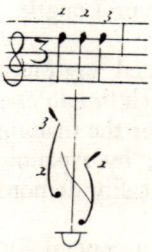

Two or more *Steps* ty'd with a double Line or Tye, are to be reckon'd only as one *Time*; as when there is three *Steps* in a *Meaſure* of *Two Times*, two of which muſt neceſſarily be ty'd with a double Tye : Which two *Steps* ſo ty'd with a double Tye, take up but one *Time*.

And if in a *Meaſure* of *Triple Time*, there happen to be four *Steps*, two of them muſt be alſo ty'd with a double Tye, as has been already ſhewn ; and for the better Explanation thereof, I have put the following Examples.

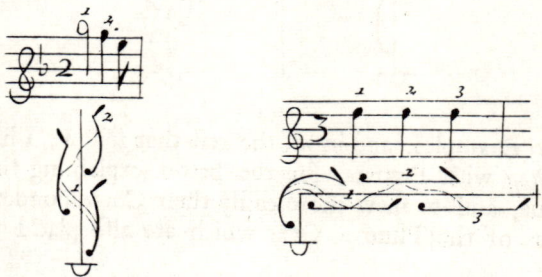

In ſhort, let it be a general Rule, that all *Steps* ty'd with a double Tye, are to be reckon'd to be only the Value of one *Time*.

Steps

Steps which have no Tye, as those which generally are alone in a *Measure*, are to be of equal Value with the *Measures* of the *Tune*; so that if one *Step* alone takes up a *Measure* of *Two Times*, or *Common Time*, that *Step* answers to the Value of the *Two Times*; and if it be to a Measure of *Triple Time*, it is then to be esteem'd as three *Times*.

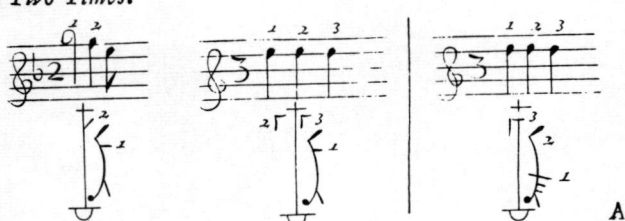

All *Steps* therefore which are alone in a Measure of either *Common* or *Triple Time*, are to be perform'd equally to the Length of the Measure of the *Tune*, except when there happens to be any Marks for the letting pass part of the Measure, as in the following Examples, where the half Measure, Crotchet, or Quaver Rests are to be reckon'd without moving, and take away from the Value of the *Step*: For if in the Measure of a *Dance* of *Two Times*, or *Common Time*, half a Measure is mark'd, it is certain the *Step* is to be reckon'd only as one *Time*, because the half Measure is for the other *Time*, during which you remain without Dancing.

Likewise if in a Measure of *Triple Time*, two Crotchet-Rests should be join'd with the *Step*, the *Step* would be reckon'd but as one *Time*, because the two Rests would take up the other two, which the Dancer ought to count, during which he stands still; and if there should be but one Rest, the *Step* would then be valu'd as *Two Times*.

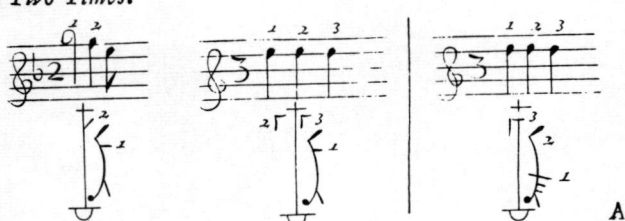

After

After having thus explain'd how each *Step* in *Dancing* agrees with the Notes in the Meafures either of *Common* or *Triple Time*, I think my felf oblig'd (the better to demonftrate what has been already fhewn) to give the Examples in the four following Pages.

In the two firft (by obferving what has been already fhewn) you will fee how the fame *Step* agrees either with a Meafure of *Two Times*, or with a Meafure of *Triple Time* ; and the two others contain each a Couplet of a *Dance*, the one to a *Tune* of *Common Time*, or *Two Times*, and the other to a *Tune* of *Triple Time*.

I fhall add, that in performing the following Couplets, you muft count the *Times* in each Meafure of the *Dance*, by the Figures there plac'd, both to the *Steps* of the *Dance*, and over the Notes of the *Tunes*, equally, and without Interruption.

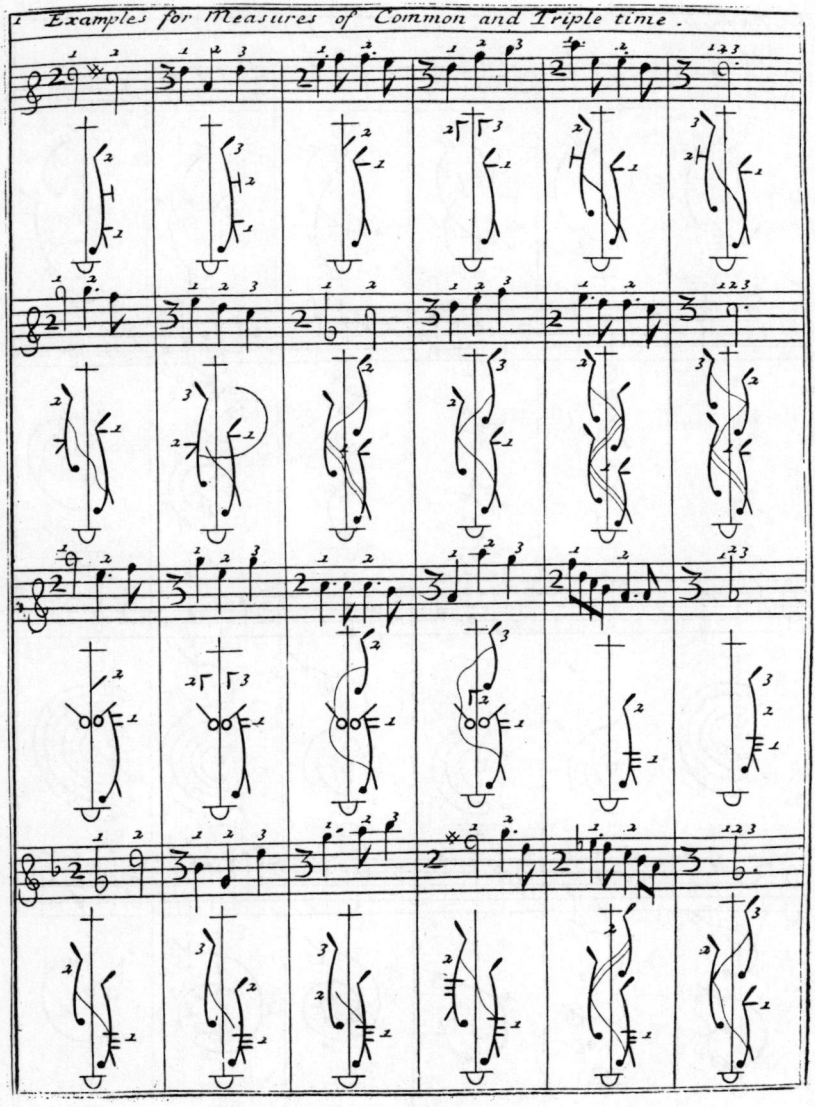

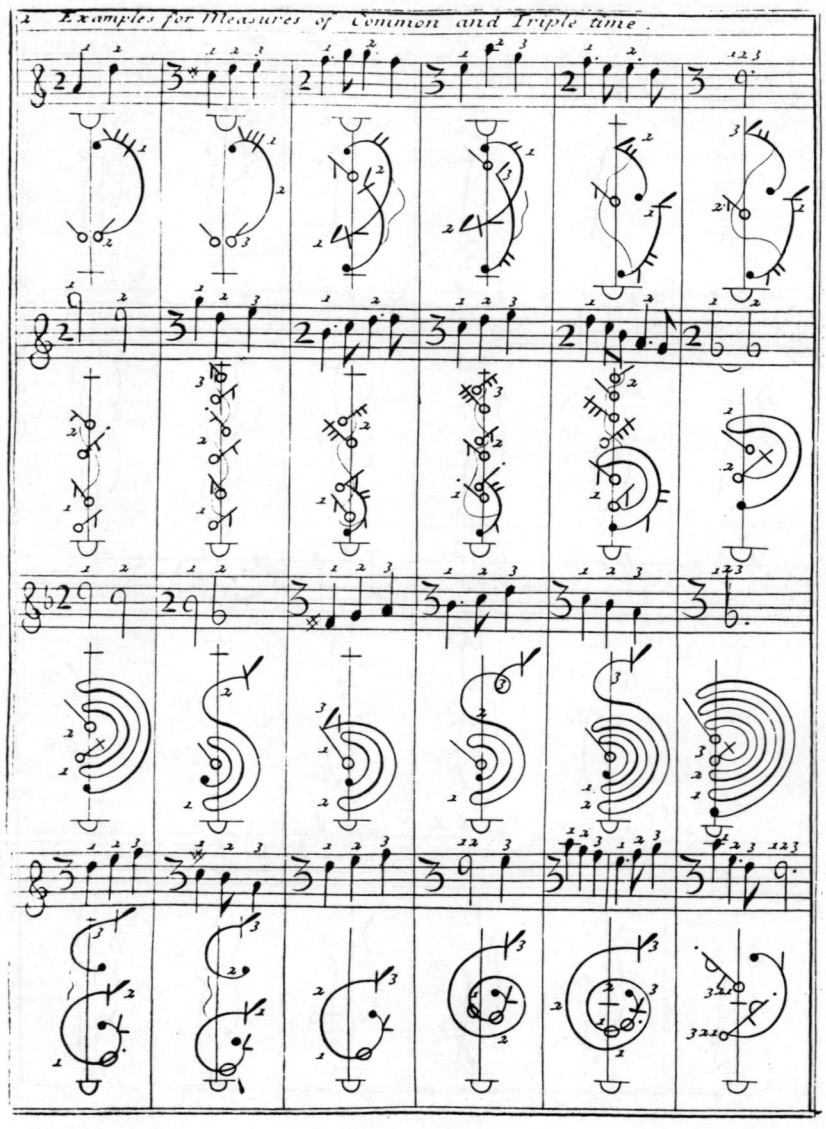

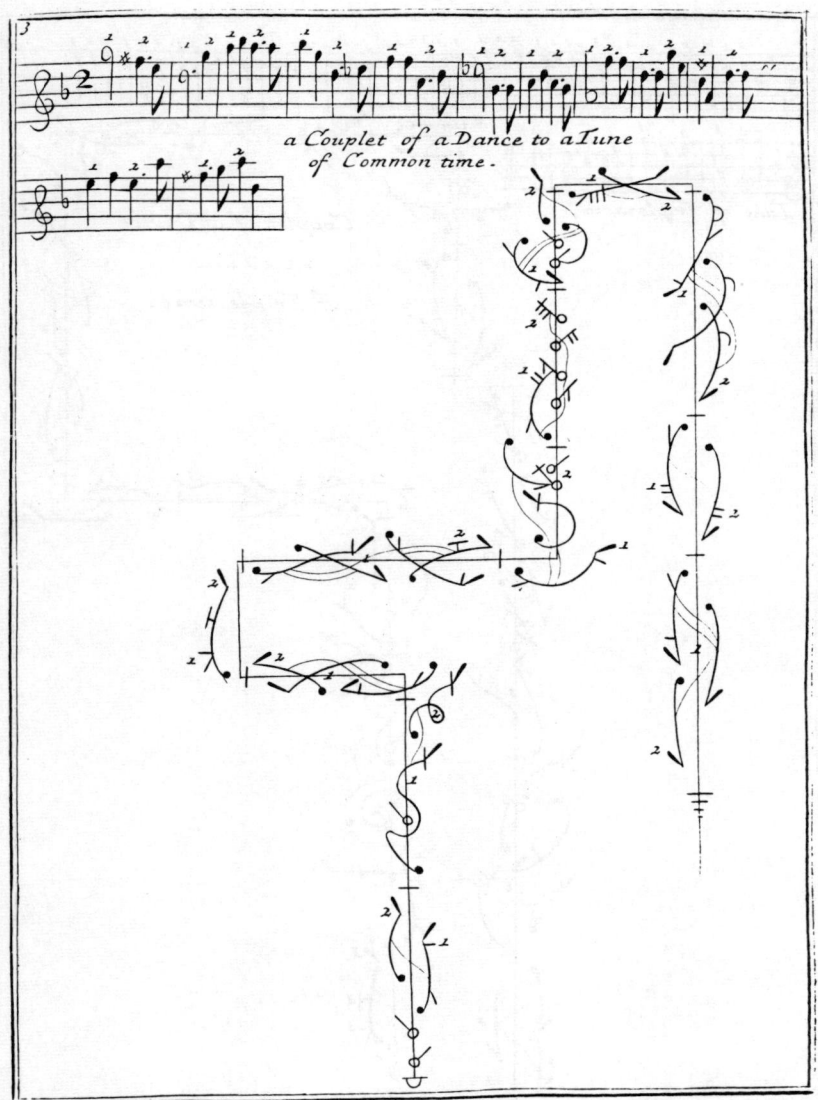

a Couplet of a Dance to a Tune
of Common time.

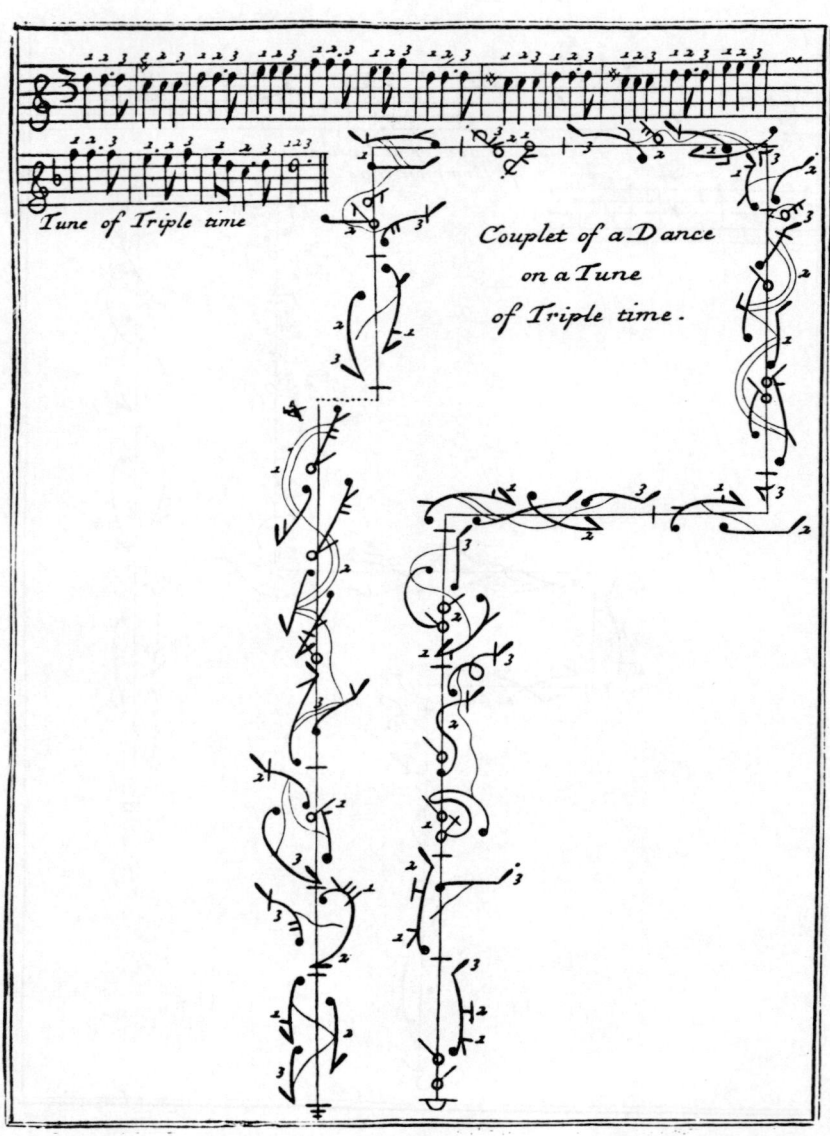

Tune of Triple time

Couplet of a Dance
on a Tune
of Triple time.

Minuett Steps	French Minuett Steps	With a Fleuret	With a Bound